CRIMINAL SENTENCING

Edited by Robert Emmet Long

THE REFERENCE SHELF

Volume 67 Number 1

The H. W. WILSON COMPANY

New York   1995

THE REFERENCE SHELF

The books in this series contain reprints of articles, excerpts from books, and addresses on current issues and social trends in the United States and other countries. There are six separately bound numbers in each volume, all of which are generally published in the same calendar year. One number is a collection of recent speeches; each of the others is devoted to a single subject and gives background information and discussion from various points of view, concluding with a comprehensive bibliography that contains books and pamphlets and abstracts of additional articles on the subject. Books in the series may be purchased individually or on subscription.

Library of Congress Cataloging-in-Publication Data

Criminal sentencing / edited by Robert Emmet Long.
     p.   cm. — (Reference shelf ; v. 67. no. 1)
   Includes bibliographical references.
   ISBN 0-8242-0868-4
   1. Criminal justice, Administration of—United States.   2. Sentences (Criminal procedure)—United States.   3. Capital punishment—United States.   4. Crime—United States.   I. Long, Robert Emmet.   II. Series.
KF9223.Z9C735   1995
345.73′0772—dc20
[347.305772]   95-2365
                                                                          CIP

Cover: A view of the Supreme Court, after hearings on school integration were held.

Photo: AP/Wide World Photos

Printed in the United States of America

CONTENTS

PREFACE

One lives in the United States today with a sense of the pervasiveness of crime. It is a plague in urban centers such as Los Angeles, which yield a daily toll of grim statistics. Undoubtedly drug trafficking involving both organized crime and inner-city street gangs of youths is a major contributor to violent crime. And the media more generally tells of a breakdown of values, including a growing lack of respect for law and order. Foreign visitors are robbed and shot to death, as in Miami; people under great stress go berserk, shooting masses of people in public places. But crime is not limited to the cities. The suburbs and small towns have become unsafe as well. Naturally, people feel a sense of outrage, and in the political arena pressure has been growing to take radical measures against crime. Conservatives have put the crime issue at the top of their agenda; and so, too, has President Clinton as shown in his recently-passed "three strikes and you are out" crime bill. But will this more aggressive stance bring about any change in the crime problem? The articles that follow offer useful background and insights into this frightening topic.

The articles in Section One focus upon crime, punishment, and youth. According to statistics the crime rate among the young has been increasing astronomically over the past few years. And, as one article points out, even fourteen-year-old children are perpetrators of the most brutal and violent crimes. Involvement in street gangs often connected with drugs combined with the shocking accessibility of guns and other weapons, help set the stage for murder carried out by these children who often end up homicide victims themselves. The question of how such children should be treated in the criminal justice system is raised in succeeding articles. Should they be tried as adults? Do so-called boot camps or shock camps work for teenage offenders? Can any of these adolescents be reclaimed? And if so, how?

Section Two concentrates on the effects of mandatory sentencing and the widespread construction of new prisons. The opening article argues that the policy of harsh mandatory sentences for drug offenders has been short-sighted. Many of those convicted of drug charges have engaged in no violent activity, and often the illegal substance involved has not been a "hard" drug but merely marijuana. Yet the sentences for such crimes have been draconian, sometimes even life imprisonment, even if only a first offense. The results of such measures have filled the prison system, and in order to accommodate violent criminals the state has had to build new facilities at considerable expense to the taxpayer. Several of the articles in this section reject the whole idea of mandatory sentences as a panacea and urge a policy of alternative sentencing for non-violent criminals as a means to ease the burden on our penal system.

Section Three deals with the reinstatement of the death penalty in many states. The article discusses the legal background of the Supreme Court's decision to lift the ban on capital punishment in 1976. Since then there has been a striking disparity in the dispensation of cases from state to state and within any single state; and it seems to the author that race is sometimes a factor when deciding who gets executed. The author argues that since the Supreme Court cannot ensure "fair and equal treatment," it should declare capital punishment unconstitutional. Other articles deal with such matters as the bias in the trial system that works against the poor and disfranchised who sometimes find themselves assigned inexperienced and even incompetent public defenders. A concluding article describes the "assembly-line" executions in the Texas state prison at Huntsville, where the state, it is disclosed, has erected barriers that make new trials practically impossible to obtain after one has once been convicted, and appeals for clemency invariably fall on deaf ears.

The final section includes the crime bill passage and Bill Clinton's 1994 State of the Union address to Congress as well as a commentary on the crime bill from *U.S. News and World Report* maintaining that neither mandatory sentencing nor increased street presence of police has ever been shown to reduce crime. Other articles focus upon the effect, now and in the future, on black neighborhoods by the disturbingly high proportion of young black men in prison, awaiting trial, or on probation.

The editor is indebted to the authors and publishers who have granted permission to reprint the materials in this compilation. Special thanks are due to Joyce Cook and the Fulton (N.Y.) Public Library staff, and to the staff of Penfield Library, State University of New York at Oswego.

ROBERT EMMET LONG

September 1994

I. ESCALATING CRIME AMONG THE YOUNG

EDITOR'S INTRODUCTION

No aspect of crime in America is more striking than the soaring crime rate among the young. The number of adolescents under the age of eighteen arrested each year for murder has increased a whopping 55 percent in the past decade. But they are not only the perpetrators of crime, they are also the victims. More adolescents now die from violence than from illnesses. Homicide, particularly by firearms, has reached epidemic proportions. It is the second leading cause of death among fifteen to nineteen year old white males, and the leading cause of death among black makes of that age group. The culture of violence as it is reflected in the young is the focus of the articles in the opening section of this volume.

In the first article, reprinted from *U.S. News & World Report*, Scott Minerbrook comments on those conditions—the sharp increase in child neglect and abuse, the arrival of crack cocaine, and availability of ever more deadly weapons in the streets—that have turned poor neighborhoods into war zones. The explosive growthof gangs, which often take the place of families that have become dysfunctional, has also exacted a fearful toll in death and maiming among the urban young. In a related article from *USA Today*, James Alex Fox and Glenn Pierce explain that by the year 2005 the number of teenagers age fifteen to nineteen will increase 23 percent, thereby bringing a further increase in crime associated with the population growth of youth. In an article reprinted from *Fortune*, Rick Tetzeli discusses programs designed to help teenagers, but the results he cites are hardly encouraging: more young black males are embroiled in the criminal justice system than are enrolled in higher education. Hanna Rosin, in a piece for the *New Republic*, notes that the principal victims of black crime are black people themselves. She goes on to comment on the campaign launched in the spring of 1994 by the Rev. Jesse Jackson, who called on young blacks to accept responsibility for their acts rather than shift blame onto racism in the criminal justice system.

In an article from *Time*, Richard Lacayo notes that around the juvenile justice system is in the process of a radical overhaul. Governor Pete Wilson of California has recently signed a bill that will permit fourteen-year-old children to be tried as adults. Not long ago Arkansas and Georgia passed similar bills in response to the soaring increase of violent crime by the very young. But the handing out of stiffer sentences to adolescents is not in itself an answer to the problem of juvenile crime. Reclaiming those youths who are reclaimable should remain a top concern of the juvenile justice system. The question of punishment versus rehabilitation is also explored in the section's concluding article, which was written by Donna Foote for *Newsweek*. Foote focuses upon the California Youth Authority, the largest juvenile justice system in the world, with a prison network housing over 9,000 youthful inmates. The Youth Training School at Chino alone houses 1,600 prisoners between the ages of eighteen and twenty-five, many convicted of homicide. Unfortunately, the article concludes, the system has practically given up on the idea of rehabilitation.

A GENERATION OF STONE KILLERS[1]

These are the reasons children are dying in America's mean streets at the hands of other children: sneakers and lambskin coats, whispers and trivial insults over menacing looks, scuffles over pocket change and, of course, drug turf. In some cases, kids are slain just for "props" (as in "proper respect")—to enhance the killer's reputation and bragging rights. Not only are the reasons unfathomably trivial but the responses of the killers are chilling; a smirk, a shrug, a cold-blooded comment. The killers are "the young and the rootless," says James Alan Fox, dean of criminal justice studies at Northeastern University. And their malign ethos has metastasized to the suburbs, where youthful murder is increasingly common.

Heartless killers and habitual criminals have always existed. But the number of killings by younger and younger kids has rarely been higher. There has been scandalously little research into the phenomenon, so experts can offer only a guess at why the

[1] Article by Scott Minerbrook from *U.S. News & World Report* Ja. 27, '94. Copyright © 1994 by U.S. News & World Report. Reprinted by permission.

number of such crimes has grown so much since the mid-1980s. They think it results from the confluence of several tragic trends: the growth of single-parent families, a sharp rise in child abuse, the arrival of crack cocaine, the escalation of weaponry on the streets, and the despair caused by the massive loss of urban manufacturing jobs. The result is an ecology of terror that has turned many poor neighborhoods into war zones. Indeed, psychologist James Garbarino, president of the Erikson Institute in Chicago, says the children of these places show many of the symptoms of kids in war-torn lands, including post-traumatic stress, emotional numbness, depression, anxiety, and rage.

A number of studies in recent years show that few of the youths who kill are psychotic. In growing up, many are animated by a chillingly rational response to an environment that is saturated with violence and stress, where it is safe to trust no one and where there is no sense of the future. In the end, these forces create literally hopeless youths subject to what Garbarino calls "terminal thinking." They believe there is nothing but woe in store for them and no solutions to problems except through aggression. Left unmitigated, these habits of mind are increasingly hard to reverse.

Here is what experts are beginning to learn about the making of this generation of stone killers:

Personality and family. Many developmental specialists agree that violence interrupts the usual growth of empathetic feelings that is necessary for moral reasoning. Ordinarily, such thinking begins at the age of three or four and comes from attachments to parents and others who teach children limits and trust and who demonstrate love and understanding. Children learn to care for others and to distinguish right from wrong at this stage by internalizing the care they receive themselves and applying it in relationships with others. "If you cut short that process with an environment of emotional chaos, the value of life and moral conduct are gone," says Charles Davenport, a psychiatrist at the Medical College of Ohio.

Many killers are the victims of awful child abuse. In a study published by the American Academy of Child and Adolescent Psychiatry in 1988, Dorothy Otnow Lewis found that 12 of 14 juveniles on death row in four states had long histories of severe beatings and sexual abuse, sometimes by drug-addicted parents. These attacks possibly caused changes in their brain chemistry and prompted violent behavior as the children grew.

In another study, released in 1992, Lewis found that maltreatment increased children's inclination to act impulsively, to be extremely wary of the world, and to exhibit "hypervigilance" to potential assaults; it predisposed them to lash out and to misperceive threats and often caused children to lose the ability to feel empathy for others. Abuse also diminished both their judgment and their verbal competence, making children less able to express what they feel or what happens to them. "If a person is chronically stressed, the biological changes that occur make them less able to control their behavior and more likely to lash out," Lewis says.

Other research suggests that witnessing violence can inspire long-term rage. Robert Pynoos, a trauma psychiatrist at the University of California at Los Angeles, has found that those who see their elders unable to control their own aggressiveness often grow up with the same untamed emotions. Sometimes, when young children witness unchecked violence against someone they know, they later fantasize about intervening to save their loved one and are furious at their inability to stop the violence. The result is that "they don't feel safe in relationships so they say, 'Why should I get into one?'" says Dr. Carl Bell of Chicago's Community Mental Health Council. "They seem glazed and indifferent when, in fact, they are imprisoned in terror."

Murderous violence rarely arises from a single, impulsive moment. Rather, it is often the culmination of years of escalating aggressive acts. The American Psychological Association and the Justice Department released separate studies last year [1993] that show several "developmental pathways" leading boys to violence. As the cruelty progresses, children develop "habits of thought" that rule out calmer ways to settle disputes, according to Ron Slaby, a developmental psychologist who teaches at Harvard University. Most commonly, it starts with stubborn behavior and defiance and progresses between the ages of eight and twelve to annoying or bullying others. Between ages twelve and fourteen, it blossoms into minor antisocial behavior like lying or shoplifting and fighting with other boys. Finally, it grows into full-blown, almost relentless violence. On the other hand, Justice Department researchers found that the brave kids who avoided getting into trouble were those who had strong parental supervision, attachments to parents, and consistent discipline.

Street pressures. No single event has contributed more to the recent contagion of violence than the wide availability of crack cocaine in American cities by the mid-to-late 1980s. It inspired the explosive growth of gangs, which became surrogate families to the emotionally wounded children of desolate communities. The lure of unimaginable wealth attracted many of the best, brightest, most enterprising, and most charismatic young men to the drug trade—and also those who looked up to them. The drug itself prompted some to kill without remorse while high and made others desperate enough to do anything to find money for the next hit. Finally, the drug profits fueled a prodigious arms race on America's streets; that led competitors to solidify markets or settle differences with an awesome toll in bloodshed.

It was inevitable that bystanders would be caught in the crossfire. A 1992 study of South Side Chicago high school students between the ages of thirteen and eighteen reported that 47 percent had seen a stabbing, 61 percent had witnessed a shooting, 45 percent had seen someone get killed, and 25 percent had experienced all three. "With these children's nerves on edge under constant threat," argues Bell, "it is clear that some will become deeply depressed, others will try to cope, and others will become perpetrators."

The menace to those trying to stay straight is frightening. Ask Sharron Corley, 19, who grew up on the mean streets of Brooklyn, N.Y., and is one of the main characters in a new book by Greg Donaldson, *The Ville*. The child of divorced parents—his father left when he was 12—Corley saw his first murder at the age of 15, when one child who felt threatened by another shot the menacing boy in the temple. Corley has dreams about being killed and those who will attend his funeral. When reminded of a recent murder of a man in his neighborhood—shot 16 times with a high-tech carbine as he lay on the ground—Corley said he had completely forgotten about it: those things happened too often for him to attach much significance to it.

National forces. Beyond family and community horrors, many experts say there are larger trends that abet the rise of coldblooded killers. There are the penal policies that allow many of the most violent criminals to return to their homes well before their sentences are served; many are treated as conquering heroes and resume their criminal ways. Then there's the easy access to handguns in many neighborhoods—even for the very young. There's an entertainment industry that each year pumps thousands of images of violence into the homes of kids who already suffer from poor or nonexistent parenting. And not least, there's the loss of millions of urban manufacturing jobs that are no longer available to kids willing to work to avoid lives of crime.

These findings highlight the need for early intervention to help children conquer their environment. Researchers have found that kids as young as seven can learn to heal themselves by telling stories about the violence they have suffered. And some experts think older kids can be turned away from crime when they are forced to confront directly what violence does to others.

The federal government recently launched massive research that will try to determine how violent behavior can be short-circuited. The results will come none too soon. By the year 2005, the number of 15-to-19-year-olds—the most violence-prone age group—will increase by 23 percent. Unless a way is found to break the vicious cycle of violence, many fear that will mean the emergence of an even larger group of stone killers.

AMERICAN KILLERS ARE
GETTING YOUNGER[2]

Buried amidst the steady stream of stories about teenage girls murdered by their obsessed boyfriends and random shootings on the streets and in the schools, the FBI actually had some good news for a change—the number of homicides in the U.S. for 1992 had fallen 6 percent over the previous year. Has the tide of violent crime in America finally been stemmed? Unfortunately for the nation, this trend will not last.

First, we caution against putting too much faith into single-year, so-called homicide trends. From year to year, murder rates can fluctuate much like the stock market. What goes up generally comes down, and what goes down generally comes up. The homicide count for 1992, although lower than that for 1991, still was above the murder toll for each of the previous 10 years.

Second, and far more important, the nation appears on the verge of a crime wave that likely will last well into the next century. Such pessimism is more than a case of "Chicken Little." Rather,

[2] Article by James Alex Fox and Glenn Pierce from *USA Today* Ja. '94. Copyright © 1994 by USA Today. Reprinted by permission of Society for the Advancement of Education.

there are some clear-cut social and demographic trends that make it very probable that today's shocking stories of drive-by shootings and fatal teenage romances will not go away. Even more disturbing is that the upsurge in killings has occurred during a period when violent crime should have been decreasing.

One of the authors (Fox) foretold nearly two decades ago, based on a predictive model developed in 1975 for his book, *Forecasting Crime Data,* that the rate of violent crime, including homicide, would decline from its 1980 peak until the early 1990s, when it would surge again. The premise then was simple. The explosion in lawlessness in the 1960s and 1970s, when violent crime escalated by double digits nearly every year, was in large part the result of demographics. During this time period, the post-World War II baby boomers—76 million strong—had reached their late adolescence and early 20s, an age when aggressive tendencies are the strongest. As they matured into adulthood during the 1980s, however, they would have outgrown their violent ways, or at least have turned to low-risk crimes of profit. More to the point, the expected decline in the size of the population most prone to violence (teens and young adults) would have translated into a reduced level of crime.

As it happened, crime reports from the early 1980s did reflect a falling rate of violence in most parts of the country. From 1980 to 1985, for instance, the U.S. homicide rate dropped 23 percent. Not surprisingly, lawmakers and police chiefs were quick to claim credit for reductions in crime levels. While various programs and policies surely had some impact, the underlying cause largely was demographic.

Then, in 1986, quite unexpectedly, things began to change for the worse. The rate of violence began to rebound, despite continued shrinkage in the population of adolescents and young adults.

The forecasting model had assumed "all else being equal," but, clearly, all else was *not* equal. Although fewer in number, the new generation—the young and the rootless—was committing violent crimes at an alarming and unprecedented rate.

The statistics are scary. Whereas the rate of homicides by adults 25 and older has continued to decline steadily, the rate among 18–24-year-olds increased 62 percent from 1986 to 1991. Even more distressing is that murder now frequently reaches down to a much younger age group—children as young as 14–17. Murder among juveniles in that age bracket increased 124 percent.

Although violence has grown among both whites and blacks, the situation is particularly acute in minority neighborhoods. Black males aged 15–24, while only one percent of the U.S. population, constitute 14 percent of the victims of homicide and 19 percent of the perpetrators.

Adolescents, particularly those in major cities, are beset with idleness and, for some, hopelessness. A growing number of teens and pre-teens see few attractive alternatives to violence, drug use, and gang membership. For them, the American dream is a nightmare. There may be little to hope for and live for, but plenty to die for and even kill for.

The causes of this reach well beyond demographics. There have been tremendous changes in the social context of crime over the past decade, which explain why this generation of youth is more violent than any other before it. As compared with their parents when they were young, this generation has more dangerous drugs in their bodies and more deadly weapons in their hands. According to the Department of Justice, an estimated one hundred thousand school children carry guns to school each day. The important role of gun availability in the increase in youth homicide can not be overstated. Since 1984, gun homicides by teenagers have tripled, while those involving other weapons have declined.

A 14-year-old armed with a gun is far more menacing than a 44-year-old with the same weapon. While the teen may be untrained in using a firearm, he is more willing to pull the trigger—without fully considering the consequences. Also, the gun psychologically distances the offender from his victim. It is all too easy—just pull the trigger. If the same teenager had to kill his victim (almost always someone he knows) with his hands, he might be deterred. Finally, the increased firepower of today's weapons have outpaced the skills of emergency room doctors to repair damage done by gunfire.

Meanwhile, Americans can not seem to unite in opposition to guns. They are told that it is impossible ever to expect a gun-free America, so why try? They are not so skeptical, however, of the "Drug-Free America" slogan. Of course, the politics of gun control and drug control are very different. It has become politically expedient for the nation's leaders to place heavy emphasis on the drug issue—often at the expense of other equally important concerns—and to suggest drugs as the basic cause behind many of the problems faced by urban America. However, drug use is a symptom, not a cause. If the U.S. somehow were to eliminate drug use, it would not necessarily reduce crime.

Above all, the most significant change in the youth population has been in attitude. This new generation of youngsters is more inclined to resort to violence over trivial issues—a pair of Nikes, a leather jacket, or even a challenging glance—or for no apparent reason. In California, for instance, two teenaged girls murdered their best friend because they were jealous of her hair.

Part of this new attitude reflects a general trend toward a reduction in moral responsibility, affecting kids and adults alike. During the 1960s and 1970s, the U.S. fought two wars—the one in Vietnam and the war against guilt. For years, Americans were told not to feel guilty—do your own thing, love the one you're with. It used to be "I'm OK, You're OK." Now it's "I'm OK, You're Dead."

Another facet of this change in attitude about violence surrounds trends in the television and movie industries. Such shows as *Hard Copy, Inside Edition,* and *A Current Affair* have replaced game shows and even the early news in many markets. Programs like *Top Cops* and *Unsolved Mysteries* dominate prime time. Television docudramas glorify criminals, transforming insignificant and obscure nobodies into national celebrities. From the standpoint of crime victims everywhere, this adds insult to injury.

Consider, for example, the publicity given the "leading men" of a band of California teenagers who called themselves the "Spur Posse" and garnered points for having sex with teenaged girls as young as 13 years of age. How proud they were describing—actually bragging—about their exploits on Jane Whitney's *Nightalk*. Adults were appalled, but these boys likely were heroes in the eyes of many 13- and 14-year-olds whose greatest desire was to grow up just like them.

Besides the glamorization of crime on television, VCRs have revolutionized the film industry—in certain respects for the worse. Concerned parents of the 1960s charged that motion pictures taught children a dangerous lesson—namely, that the consequences of violence are temporary and trivial. Injury and death typically were presented in a sanitized manner.

In terms of body counts, movies of today are no more violent than their counterparts 25 years ago, but their portrayal of murder no longer leaves anything to the imagination. The consequences of violence routinely are depicted as graphically as possible, without regard for how they may affect impressionable

young viewers. Thanks to video cassettes, children can replay
their favorite gory scenes over and over.

Parents now have a much more difficult problem—how to
keep their offspring from becoming totally desensitized to human misery, mayhem, and murder. Because of the steady diet of
gory films to which they are exposed, children of the 1990s slowly,
but surely, are growing more tolerant of the effects of violence.
They no longer are repulsed by stories of extreme brutality, even
when they are real. As one teenaged bystander remarked following the 1992 murder of an MIT student, "Hey, what's the big
deal . . . people die every day."

While negative socializing forces—such as drugs, guns, gangs,
television, and movies—have grown more powerful, the positive
forces of family, school, church, and community have grown
weaker. The decline in these forms of support reflects a pervasive
disinvestment in American youth over the last 30 years, docu-
mented in Glenn Pierce's *Disinvestment in America's Children and
Youth.*

Social and economic changes in society, in two related respects, have diminished the contribution of women to child-
rearing and socialization. As women have entered the labor force
in greater numbers, they have had less time for their families,
have been less able to participate in the broad range of voluntary
organizations that in the past strengthened local communities,
and have been less able to supervise youngsters (both their own
and their neighbors') within their day-to-day activities. Equally
important, as professional opportunities have opened up for fe-
males in the workforce, highly qualified women, who at one time,
for lack of other options, would have gone into teaching or child
care, are more likely to seek careers in law, medicine, and science.

Increasingly, kids are being raised in homes disrupted by divorce or economic stress; too many emerge undersocialized and
undersupervised. This is not to imply any level of blame on parents, and mothers in particular. Most parents are well-meaning
and would like to have a greater role in their children's lives, if
only they could. However, many families lack the support to control and guide their offspring.

Compensating for the Void

American society has not addressed the issue of how to compensate for the void left by changes in the status of women and

their entry into the labor market. Society no longer can rely al-most totally on the unpaid and/or underpaid time of women to socialize and supervise the nation's youth. The government has not stepped forward in the form of child care programs and better schools; the private sector has dragged its feet in parental leave and child care programs; and many men have not taken on a greater share of parenting and household responsibilities.

As a consequence of changes in the family and lack of alterna-tive support programs for youth, children spend too little time engaged in structured activity with positive role models and too much time "hanging out" or watching savage killings on TV. The effects of the over-all disinvestment in youth are being felt in several alarming respects—increased rates of high-risk behavior among youth, from violence to drug use; reduced levels of psy-chological well-being, from suicide to psychiatric commitments; and lowering of academic preparedness and achievement.

At this point in time, the U.S. is due for a demographic double-whammy. Not only are violent teens maturing into even more violent young adults, but they are being succeeded by a new and larger group of teenagers. The same massive baby boom generation that, as teenagers, produced a crime wave in the 1970s has grown up and had children of their own. This "baby boomer-ang" cohort of youngsters now is reaching adolescence.

By the year 2005, the number of teenagers aged 15–19 will increase by 23 percent, which undoubtedly will bring additional increases in crime and other social ills associated with overpopula-tion of youth. The population growth will be even more pro-nounced among minorities. For example, the amount of 15–19-year-olds will rise 28 percent among blacks and 47 percent among Hispanics. Given that a large number of these children often grow up in conditions of poverty, many more teenagers will be at risk in the years ahead.

The challenge for the future, therefore, is how best to deal with youth violence—and there is little reason for optimism. America seems to be obsessed with easy solutions that won't work, such as the wholesale transfer of juveniles to the jurisdiction of the adult court or even imposing the death penalty, at the expense of difficult solutions that will work, such as providing pre-teens with strong, positive role models and quality schools.

State legislatures around the country have responded to con-cerns about the rising number of juvenile killings, often over-reacting to certain highly publicized cases of brutal and senseless murder involving teens. In recent years, most states have made it easier—even automatic—to try juvenile killers as adults. Ignoring the immaturity of a 15- or 16-year-old, lawmakers have accepted the idea that murder is an adult crime and thus deserves an adult punishment.

Clearly, there are certain youths who are beyond the reach of the juvenile system—repeat violent offenders who are not amenable to the rehabilitative orientation of the juvenile system. On a case-by-case basis, these kids selectively should be handled outside the juvenile domain. Yet, in the effort to appear tough on crime, legislatures are making it too easy to waive youthful offenders into an adult system that is ill-prepared to handle them.

The national trend toward trying juveniles as adults in order to incarcerate them longer may address the need for justice and retribution, but it can not be counted on for dissuading kids from the temptations and thrill of street crime and gang membership. No matter how punitive society becomes and what kind or how strong of a message is sent out to the street, teens who are attracted to crime always will turn a deaf ear to deterrence. Besides, by the time a juvenile offender has "graduated" to murder, it is likely too late to reach him.

Instead, attention must be focused on the primary grades, when youngsters still are impressionable and interested in what teachers and other authority figures have to say. As Denver District Attorney Norman S. Early, Jr., maintains, "I would rather build the child than rebuild the adult."

The nation must reinvest in youth and strive to make legitimate activity more attractive than criminal behavior. This will take time, hard work, and an awful lot of money. It is well known that positive reinforcement for pro-social behavior always will outperform punishment for anti-social behavior. Besides, it is far cheaper to hire elementary grade teachers and pay them commensurate with the importance of the job than it is to build more prisons and hire more correctional officers later.

Tragically for America, it is unlikely that proposals focused on youngsters and pre-teens will attract much political momentum. Most politicians need to show results within four years in order to get re-elected. For them, there remains a far more immediate political payoff in advocating the "new three-R's"—retribution, retaliation, and revenge—attempting to convince voters that they are tough on crime.

MOST DANGEROUS AND ENDANGERED[3]

When Detroit announced a plan to open three all-male, all-black public schools last year, the National Organization for Women and the American Civil Liberties Union rose up and defeated it. In response the Board of Education allotted 130 places in the three academies to girls. But the word went out in the community: don't send your daughters. And when Ray Johnson, administrator of the Paul Robeson Academy, opened his doors in September, 146 of his 160 students, preschoolers through second-graders, were boys. Says he: "That shows you the will and the power of the community. They know that business as usual isn't working."

Business as usual *isn't* working. Bluntly put, boys are in crisis. A few of the grim statistics: firearm homicide is the second leading cause of death for boys 15 to 19 years old, after car crashes. At least 120,000 teens became fathers in 1989. Unemployment among teen boys is 25.4 percent, up from 15.5 percent four years ago. Though the crisis is by no means confined to African American youths, it is most acute among them: an estimated 40 percent fail to graduate from big-city high schools; more black men are embroiled in the criminal justice system than are enrolled in higher education.

The financial consequences of the crisis are severe. The federal government spent over $25 billion in 1990 on health and social services for families begun by teen mothers. The cost of treating gunshot wounds was an estimated $863 million in 1985, the most recent year for which figures are available, and that was before the recent escalation in violence. Ron Mincy, a sociologist at the nonpartisan Urban Institute, says the country has spent some $20 billion in the past few years building prisons mostly to house young African American men. "Nobody's calculus makes sense of that number," he says. "We do treat people who fall through the cracks—girls in welfare, boys in prison—but it would be cheaper if we went back earlier in the life cycle and asked what we want adolescents to accomplish."

Schools, hospitals, and groups funded by government and

[3] Article by Rick Tetzeli from *Fortune* Ag. 10, '92. Copyright © 1992 by Fortune. Reprinted by permission.

business are beginning to address that question. Programs that target males from high-risk backgrounds—those in low-income, single-parent families, from neighborhoods where economic prospects are minimal and boys are faced with gangs, drug dealing, and soaring rates of violence—are trying to get to the boys before the trouble starts.

Child development experts believe the preschool and junior high years are particularly critical. Head Start, which has achieved short-term success in preparing low-income boys and girls for school, is everyone's favorite early childhood development program. But a recent study by J. S. Fuerst, professor of social welfare policy at Loyola University in Chicago, suggests that for boys the gains from early childhood programs don't last. Fuerst looked at the Chicago Child Parent Centers, six public schools that combined heavy parental involvement with a highly structured learning program for at-risk kids. One school took in preschoolers at age three and stayed with them through sixth grade; the other five went only through third grade.

The results of Fuerst's study are discouraging. Only 49 percent of the boys who attended the schools that went through third grade graduated from high school, compared with 40 percent of boys in a similarly disadvantaged group that received no preschool education at all. When boys stayed through the sixth grade, however, 70 percent graduated. Says Fuerst: "We've been breaking our backs patting ourselves on the back over the success of Head Start. If funding is limited, we should focus on low-income and minority families *and* give them an extended period of exposure, especially for boys."

Jacquelynne Eccles, a professor of child psychology at the University of Michigan, identifies characteristics shared by 10- to 13-year-old kids at risk: low self-confidence, low grades, a history of trouble in school, and strained relationships with their fathers in many cases. Boys grow more anxious about performing poorly in school, especially if the future seems dim. Eccles sees a growing number of such boys in the suburban southeast Michigan communities she has been studying. Says she: "Their families have worked for generations in the Detroit factories. This is the first generation of boys who can't count on that. The payoff for education is not as clear to them as it was to their parents."

Detroit's academies, the closest thing in the country to all-male, all-black public schools, represent an attempt to provide the kind of continuing support Fuerst calls for, though many educators and other experts dislike the way they do it. This fall the Paul Robeson Academy will move into its own building and add a third grade; eventually it will serve kids through the eighth grade. Building self-esteem is a central goal, as is providing boys with male role models: unlike those in most elementary schools, many of the teachers are men. Discipline in the small classes is strong, and the curriculum is demanding, with math, science, social studies, English, and French all taught beginning in preschool. Students are expected to live by the seven principles of unity, self-determination, collective work and responsibility, cooperative economics, purpose, creativity, and faith. Says administrator Johnson: "I'm not interested in any candy-coated, kiddy-cute kind of education playing with building blocks."

Parental involvement is high, and parents who attended a June graduation ceremony are happy with the school. Says Betty Pettaway, mother of a six-year-old kindergartener, Winzell: "I like the structure of how they teach little boys to be men. Now when he acts up at home, I say, 'Is that a Paul Robeson boy?' and he checks himself." Adds Deborah Brooks, single mother of seven-year-old Hakim: "I work in the records office at a prison, and one thing I find is how many of the men there come from broken homes where they didn't have a male figure to look up to. This will help him out a great deal."

More fathers seem to be recognizing their own importance. A 1991 study by Du Pont showed that 35 percent of male employees wanted a transition time to care for a newborn, vs. 15 percent who felt that way in 1986. Terry Thompson, 34, a single father who works as a mail service agent at Du Pont's headquarters in Wilmington, Delaware, arranged with his boss to work at home for a month after the birth of his son, Marcus, in May. "The baby's mother and I decided I would be the one to raise him," he says. "I worked when the baby was sleeping, which means I put in some really weird hours, but the work did get done. I felt it was really important that I be there at the beginning for Marcus. I know if I don't raise him, the streets will, and I don't want that."

While Detroit will expand its academy system to ten schools next fall, many experts believe that all-male, all-black schools send the wrong message to African American boys. Says Jewelle Taylor Gibbs, a child psychologist at the University of California at Berkeley and editor of *Young, Black, and Male in America: An Endangered Species:* "We are telling these boys that there's something so wrong with you that you can't learn in a regular environment.

Furthermore, we're resegregating the schools, and I'm totally opposed to that."

In truth, few supporters of such schools see them as the only way to teach African American youth. Says the Urban Institute's Mincy: "I view them as one of a number of initiatives we can construct to learn about serving young black males." He adds: "Liberals have compassion for low-income and minority populations, but they also have feminism in their bones, and that makes it impossible for them to admit that boys and girls are different. That's a political issue I'm not interested in. I want to know what we're going to do to close the gaps between black males and white males and between black males and black women."

Those gaps are often wide. According to the Bureau of Labor Statistics, 47 percent of black males between 16 and 19 are unemployed this summer, vs. 36 percent of black girls and 22 percent of white boys.

Mentors have traditionally offered beneficial role models for many boys. Recognizing this, the Federal National Mortgage Association (Fannie Mae) launched the highly successful Futures 500 program at Washington, D.C.'s Woodside High School three years ago. Boys and girls who get all A's and B's are awarded $500 per semester toward college tuition and assigned a Fannie Mae employee mentor. One effect, says salutatorian Jonathan Pinckney, 18, a Futures 500 member, is that the traditional role of inner-city peer groups has been turned on its head at Woodside. It's hard for other students to argue with successful teens who are going on field trips with their mentors and earning money for good grades. Says he: "The students who succeed are no longer looked down upon, and the others want to be a part of it, even if they don't verbally communicate the idea."

That fact illustrates an important point: mentoring works best when group dynamics reinforce the effect. Ron Mincy says, "Trying to change the thinking and behavior of black youth by operating on the individual is foolish. We have to operate with the peer group."

Preventive interventions, like some sex education programs for inner-city youth, are finding the same thing: working with groups of boys is the best way to break down cultural myths they inherit from peers. This is especially crucial for 10- to 15-year-old boys, who begin to look up to older boys more than they do to whatever parents may be around.

Since 1990 the Male Adolescent Program at Rush Presbyterian Center St. Luke's Hospital in Chicago has led small groups of sixth- through eighth-grade boys—most from low-income, broken homes—in weekly hour-long sessions that combine math and reading with learning about sexual responsibility. Social workers lead discussions provoked by the boys' questions, such as, "What do I do if a girl offers to have sex with me, and I know she's done it with a bunch of my friends?" The boys themselves came up with pros and cons to consider in answering the question.

The 55 boys in the program the first year all passed on to the next grade, and none became fathers. Says program director Stephen Gillenwater: "That's highly unusual for this population. These kids are stuck. They hear that if they're going to be men they have to have sex. On the other hand, their parents have told them not to have a kid, without any details as to how to prevent it." Typically boys turn to older peers for sexual information—or misinformation. "When we started, there was a myth around the sixth-graders on the West Side that ear wax would keep a girl from getting pregnant. If she jumps when you put ear wax on her, she's got a sexually transmitted disease."

According to the nonprofit Alan Gutmacher Institute, 72 percent of American boys lose their virginity by age 19, and 33 percent by 16. Largely because of AIDS, condom use has doubled since 1982. Some 66 percent of sexually active black males between 15 and 19, and 54 percent of whites, say they used a condom the last time they had sex.

AIDS isn't the only reason safety makes sense. Prospects for young fathers of every color are terrible. Fewer than 25 percent of teen fathers are married to their child's mother at the child's birth, and 62 percent of those drop out of high school. Yet for some boys fatherhood still looks like a shortcut to adulthood. Chris Hoopiiaina, 17, met his wife, Claudia, 18, two years ago, when he was rigging the stage for her dance class at Granite High School in Salt Lake City. They married last September, and Claudia gave birth to their son, Colton, in January. Chris says they planned the baby: "We just wanted to get out and experience our lives. This way we'll still be young when Colton is growing up."

But being a father has been more than Chris bargained for. The Hoopiiainas moved into their own apartment when Colton was born. Now they're $3,000 in debt and back living with his folks. Says Chris: "We spent our money on fast-food restaurants and movies, and I bought a stereo. There was no money for rent because we were just throwing it away on stupid things." Both

Chris and Claudia have dropped out of school and are working full time: Chris takes orders at Burger King, and Claudia waits on customers at Arby's. His mother and stepfather take care of Colton when they're working. According to their plan, eventually Chris will start working two jobs to put Claudia through college, then she'll put him through college.

Chris finds help in a support group for fathers at the University of Utah Medical Center Teen Mother and Child Program, funded in part by US West. Once a month teen fathers like Chris get together to vent frustrations and trade tips on parenting. Says he: "We need all the help we can get. You wouldn't believe how good it feels to talk to someone who's going through what you're going through."

Such support groups are becoming more common, and the demand is growing. According to Nancy Hale Stewart, a social worker at the Salt Lake City clinic, more couples are coming in now without basic necessities like food and shelter, and without support from their parents. Also disturbing is that more teens say they planned their child. Says Chris: "Around here it looks like the Nineties are going to be the Pregnancy Hall of Fame." Several of the Hoopiiainas' friends have become pregnant after seeing Chris and Claudia still together and happy. Says he: "They began to admire us and think they might be proud to be parents too. I feel miserable about it. They don't have any clue what it's like."

A better ticket to adulthood is a job. Joe Swift, 16, was four years old when his father went to prison for killing Joe's mother. After moving around a great deal and living with different family members, Joe finally wound up in the New Life Youth Services rehabilitation facility in Montgomery County, Pennsylvania, after pleading guilty to grand theft auto. With the help of an auto mechanics teacher there, Joe decided to turn his life around. Says he: "I decided to stop vandalizing cars and start fixing them."

When Joe got out in May 1990, New Life placed him with a foster mother in a trailer park in Green Lane, Pennsylvania, where he and four of his friends repair neighbors' cars and motorcycles. This August he starts a two-year apprenticeship in metalworking at Cook Specialty Co. He'll work two days a week at the metal parts fabricator and spend three days a week at a local technical school, where his classroom courses will be tailored to his work experience.

Cook Specialty CEO Tom Panzarella is proud of his company's reputation, which Xerox burnished in January by honoring the company as one of its 32 "certified parts suppliers" world-wide. Why would Panzarella put that reputation on the line with a boy like Joe? He responds: "Are we going to condemn a kid for life because of past problems?"

Taking that kind of chance is one way business can help boys with the odds against them. Poised and confident, Joe seems more than ready to handle new responsibilities. Of the many boys who applied for internships at Cook, he scored highest on the me-chanical aptitude test. His street smarts and savvy also greatly impressed the boss. Says Panzarella: "It wasn't 'Let's do this for the good of Joe.' He can be an excellent employee and a real leader, if he wants it."

James Comer, a child psychiatrist at Yale who has worked in inner cities for years, says we can't wait any longer to address the economic and social issues that keep disadvantaged boys, espe-cially inner-city minorities, from entering the mainstream. "It's getting late," he says. "I look at the year 2000 as a psychological watershed. If we don't put some things in place by then, we'll be on a precipitous downward slope." For every boy like Joe Swift, many more don't get much encouragement to break out of their often desperate situations. Others see little incentive to avoid fighting, stealing, leaving school, creating babies, doing drugs, or taking other legal and economic risks that can cause much misery later. Programs like those described here try to supply such en-couragement and incentive; their basic message to boys should be heeded, too, by a country that wants to help them: as Joe puts it, "The future depends on now."

ACTION JACKSON[4]

On the bleachers of a freezing auditorium at Phelps Career High School in Washington, D.C., hundreds of students huddled in their winter coats one February morning, and listened to May-or Sharon Pratt Kelly talk dryly about "the city's commitment to investing in our schools." Then, as the keynote speaker swept into the room, Kelly was overwhelmed in midsentence by the roar of

[4] Article by Hanna Rosin from *The New Republic* Mr. 21, '94. Copyright © 1994 by The New Republic. Reprinted by permission.

"Jesse, Jesse, Jesse!" Within minutes, the students were on their feet. "Repeat after me," said Jesse Jackson. "I am somebody. We shall be made safer. We shall save each other. We shall give our babies the dignity of our names." When they sat back down they were alert. "The dope-pusher won't stop pushing. You've got to change your mind. You have the power to study three hours a night, not to engage in sex without love and make unwanted babies, not to kill somebody, not to consume drugs. It's a matter of self-respect." When a group of boys acted up for the cameramen, he scolded, "Don't be on T.V. in front of white folks and make us look crazy. This is a serious session." By the end of the hour the kids had taken over the mike, asking the mayor not only for heat, but for computers and new textbooks.

In high schools and churches across the country, in press conferences and congressional hearings in Washington, Jackson has been redefining "black-on-black" crime as "the No. 1 civil rights issue," claiming it "robs our movement of its moral authority." Not surprisingly, his message of self-empowerment is received cynically by many who see it merely as his latest ploy for the spotlight. After all, only six months ago D.C.'s shadow senator was calling District statehood "the most important civil rights and social justice issue in America today."

Well, sometimes cynicism about Jackson isn't entirely justified. The truth is, Jackson has broken a taboo that has silenced black leaders for decades every place outside their churches; he is admonishing the community openly, before black and white audiences, about individual responsibility for inner-city crime. And his dose of conservative moral rectitude has eased the way for black leaders outside the traditional civil rights community—such as the Congressional Black Caucus and city mayors—to fashion constructive, preventive antidotes to prevailing hard-line crime policies such as "three strikes and you're out."

Jackson's crusade is based on some alarming realities. For all the hoopla in the national press, there is no crime crisis in America—unless you're black. Despite one-third of Americans rating crime as their biggest problem, crime as a whole has been steadily decreasing since 1981, according to Bureau of Justice statistics. But not in the black community. From 1968 to 1984 white murder victims increased about 10 percent, which, factoring in population growth, is actually a decrease. In contrast, the murder rate among blacks increased 65 percent. A black person is now seven times as likely to be murdered, four times as likely to be raped, three times as likely to be robbed and twice as likely to be assaulted or have a car stolen. The total number of murders—about 22,000 last year—has remained constant since 1980; they now just disproportionately affect the black community. America's average murder victim is a black boy between the ages of 12 and 15; 95 percent of the time his murderer is another black boy or man. "More young black men die each year from gunshots than the total who have died from lynchings in the entire history of the United States," Jackson says. "We have become our own worst enemy." It's hard to put it more starkly than that.

Jackson is doing more than just giving speeches. In January [1994] he organized a three-day conference of black leaders in Washington called "Stop the Violence. Save Our Children," which has since been replicated in several cities. While short on specific solutions, the conference provided a high-profile platform for discussions that have traditionally remained behind closed doors. In one session on violence against women, C. Delores Tucker of the National Political Congress of Black Women held up enlarged copies of the cartoon insert in rapper Snoop Doggy Dog's album, which shows a faceless, bikini-clad woman, referred to only as "BEEITCH," being kicked out of bed. Eleanor Holmes Norton, D.C.'s representative, chaired the session on welfare reform, and warned that "it would be disastrous for black people to have an automatic anti-reform posture."

Recently, Jackson unveiled an anti-crime program called "Reclaim Our Youth," which relies on one hundred churches in one hundred cities to mentor ten first-time, nonviolent offenders each. These are kids who would otherwise sit in jail for months awaiting trial and picking up bad habits. In D.C., which will serve as the model, Jackson has been meeting with planning groups—including federal judges and prosecutors—every Thursday since June. After each high school lecture, he makes kids sign pledges not to take drugs or carry weapons, and to tell on those who do. He then lines up those over 18 to register them to vote. He also asks parents to sign a pledge to pick up report cards and meet with teachers, a goal Clinton touted in his State of the Union address after a half-hour meeting with Jackson the day before the speech.

In an era where "there is no more drama of mass marches," Jackson describes his role, immodestly, as a "catalyst, a visionary," and leaves it up to black elected officials to carry out his vision. How far they can go, however, is an open question. After all, implementing Jackson's strategy means criticizing the very people who put them in office. Nevertheless, there is movement. "We need to return to the basic values that got us through four hundred years of the sojourn from slavery," said Kweisi Mfume, chairman of the Congressional Black Caucus, at Jackson's conference. "Our survival has continued but not our development. We need not government intervention, but a basic respect for life." Baltimore Mayor Kurt Schmoke, a former federal and state prosecutor, put it more simply: "I could use more cops on my streets."

This Jackson-led shift is the good news. The bad news is, it's not always there. For example, the alternative crime bill, sponsored by the Congressional Black Caucus, is still mired in old-think. Aside from a couple of tough provisions (more cops, boot camps), the bill's sponsors have taken a rhetorical stance against any kind of punishment; they have been content to hide behind what they call a racist justice system. Mfume has dismissed all prisons as "an antiquated approach to crime." Witnesses in the House hearings on the bill gave boilerplate speeches about racism in arrest and sentencing patterns. One CBC aide called the bill's Racial Justice Act, which corrects for disparities in sentencing for crack and cocaine offenses and in applying the death penalty, "the most important part of the bill."

This reversion to paleoliberalism isn't simply lamentable on its own terms, it is also bad politics. The CBC runs the risk of being ignored in the crime debate, when it could have found a way to be center-stage. There's a danger even that its more modest—and defensible—prevention programs, such as Head Start and a summer jobs program, could be lost as a result. With 150 moderate Democrats poised to pass some bill in the next month, CBC members would do better to join the final compromise and avoid giving the bargaining power to House Republicans. (They have exacerbated their marginalization by telling the Judiciary Committee they will automatically oppose any bill that includes new mandatory minimum or death penalty provisions, both of which have solid support in the House.) By participating, they might be able to squeeze more money for Head Start and narrow the scope of the death penalty and mandatory minimum provisions.

The old-style rhetoric also erodes the progress made in breaking the silence on black crime. Blaming crime on racism in the justice system—rather than calling a criminal a criminal—unwittingly perpetuates the stereotype of the whole black community as having criminal potential; a better strategy would recognize that black people are overwhelmingly the victims of crime—as Jackson does by calling his crusade a "victims-led revolution"—and deal with the criminals harshly. "It's the negative side of black unity," says writer Stanley Crouch. "Ninety-nine percent of us are not criminals, and we have to rid these monsters among us. Let them shoot up the CBC and we'll see what happens in the next crime bill."

The CBC rhetoric has its echoes elsewhere. Mayor Kelly, whom Jackson chose to moderate the Rainbow Coalition conference's session on solutions, posed the problem of crime in terms too daunting for anyone to solve. After warning against letting "a bunch of talking heads come up with programs," she added this: "I want to make one last observation. . . . It's not just exclusively our problem. The loss of values is in every racial segment. Nowadays we are preyed upon by organized drug activity on America, where rarely African Americans are at the helm of any of it. We are preyed upon by people who make a living selling guns. This is a capitalist enterprise that criss-crosses America." (No wonder she called in the National Guard to combat violence last year.) Reverend Al Sharpton, the Rainbow Coalition's director in New York, agrees. "The real criminals are the gun manufacturers that are inundating our communities with guns," he says. "Snoop Dog didn't put those guns there." The specter of a massive capitalist onslaught gets even more abstract as the real criminal is identified as the evil box in our homes. "Channel 2, *Murder She Wrote*. Channel 4, *Terminator 3*. Channel 7, *Throw Your Momma Off the Train*. That's what taught young people how to be violent," Sharpton intoned in the introduction to a Nation of Islam crime conference in December [199]. To them, Jackson has a simple answer: "Whatever happens, you say the devil made me do it. Pharaoh's dead, so stop talking about The Man."

WHEN KIDS GO BAD[5]

Frank Jackson knows something about violent crime. As head of the Dangerous Offenders Task Force in Wake County, North

---

[5] Article by Richard Lacayo from *Time* S. 19, '94. Copyright © 1994 by Time Inc. Reprinted by permission.

Carolina, he's been around his share. Even so, this tape makes him cringe. It's a 911 call made to police the night of July 27 [1994]. A young woman is phoning for help from her apartment in Fuquay-Varina, about 15 miles from Raleigh. Just before the tape goes dead—police believe the phone was ripped from the wall—she can be heard screaming, "Don't harm my baby!" Jackson knows what happened next. Over the next several minutes she was beaten bloody with a mop handle and raped. The attacker was a neighbor who had apparently become infatuated with her. The woman, who survived, is 22. The accused rapist, Andre Green, is 13.

Green will be the first youthful offender tried under a North Carolina law passed earlier this year that permits children as young as 13 to be tried as adults. If convicted of rape, Green, who confessed to the crime but has no previous criminal record, will not be eligible for parole for 20 years. Jackson, who will prosecute the case, thinks Green is somebody who can't be let off lightly. He also wonders if lengthy confinement won't make Green worse. "It's kind of scary to think what kind of monster may be created," Jackson says. "He could be released at the age of 33 after having been raised in the department of corrections with some of the most hardened criminals North Carolina has to offer."

The American juvenile-justice system was designed one hundred years ago to reform kids found guilty of minor crimes. Increasingly these days, the system is overwhelmed by the Andre Greens, by pint-size drug runners and by 16-year-old gunmen. The response on the part of lawmakers has been largely to siphon the worst of them out of that system by lowering the age at which juveniles charged with serious crimes—usually including murder, rape, and armed assault—can be tried in adult courts. Last week California Governor Pete Wilson signed a bill lowering the threshold to 14. Earlier this year Arkansas did the same, and Georgia decided that youths from the ages of 14 through 17 who are charged with certain crimes will be tried as adults automatically. This being election time, candidates around the country are engaged in a kind of reverse auction to see who would send even younger felons to the adult system. Fourteen? Why not 13? Why not 12?

Even if the spectacle of politics coming to grips with pathology is not pretty, who can deny that when eleven-year-olds like Robert ("Yummy") Sandifer kill or when a 14-year-old drives nails into the heels of a younger boy—a recent episode from Somerset,

Pennsylvania—there is good reason to be unnerved? A breeding ground of poverty and broken families and drugs and guns and violence, real or just pictured, has brought forth a violent generation. "We need to throw out our entire juvenile-justice system," says Gil Garcetti, the District Attorney of Los Angeles County, whose biggest headache, after the O. J. trial, is the city's youth gangs. "We should replace it with one that both protects society from violent juvenile criminals and efficiently rehabilitates youths who can be saved—and can differentiate between the two."

During the past six years, there has been a significant increase in juvenile crime in the most serious categories: murder, rape, robbery, and aggravated assault. Homicide arrests of kids ages 10 through 14 rose from 194 to 301 between 1988 and 1992. In 1986 a majority of cases in New York City's Family Court were misdemeanors; today more than 90 percent are felonies. Though killers under the age of 15 are still relatively rare—over the past three years in L.A., for instance, those 14 or younger accounted for just 17 of the 460 homicides committed by kids under 18—younger kids are increasingly involved in deadlier crime. "There is far more gratuitous violence and far more anger, more shooting," says Judge Susan R. Winfield, who presides over the Family Division of the Washington, D.C., Superior Court. "Youngsters used to shoot each other in the body. Then in the head. Now they shoot each other in the face."

Gunfire has become sufficiently common in and around classrooms, mostly in the inner city, that an astonishing number of schools have started to treat their own corridors as potential crime scenes. Some are tearing out lockers to deny hiding places for handguns or banning carryalls and bookbags for the same reason.

No segment of society is immune to the problem. The most famous youthful offenders of the 1990s, Erik Menendez, at 19, of Beverly Hills, California, and Amy Fisher, at 17, of Merrick, Long Island, came from mostly white communities of nice houses. But it's in the inner cities where an interlocking universe of guns, gangs, and the drug trade has made mayhem a career path for kids and equipped them with the means to do maximum damage along the way. Children involved in the drug trade get guns to defend themselves against older kids who want their money. For the ones still on a piggy-bank budget, the streets offer rent-a-guns for $20 an hour. Who can be surprised, then, that on a typical day last year about 100,000 juveniles were in lockup across the country?

With the omnibus crime bill that just squeezed through Congress, the Federal Government made its partial gesture toward a solution. Under the new law, it's a crime for juveniles to possess a handgun or for any adult to transfer one to them except in certain supervised situations. It also provides for programs—like those that keep schools open later—intended to discourage kids from finding trouble.

Those were the very provisions that some Republicans denounced as "pork." Yet while crime control can be one of the most contentious issues in American life, there is something resembling an emerging ideological consensus on one thing: some kids are beyond help. You can hear it even when talking with Attorney General Janet Reno, who believes crime has its roots among neglected children. She still stresses the need for "a continuum" of government attention that begins with prenatal care and includes the school system, housing authorities, health services, and job-training programs. But she also recognizes that the continuum will sometimes end in an early jail cell. "It's imperative for serious juvenile offenders to know they will face a sanction," she says. "Too many of them don't understand what punishment means because they have been raised in a world with no understanding of reward and punishment."

A consensus is also developing about the juvenile-justice system. It takes forever to punish kids who seriously break the law, and it devotes far too much time and money to hardened young criminals while neglecting wayward kids who could still be turned around. "We can't look a kid in the eye and tell him that we can't spend a thousand dollars on him when he's 12 or 13 but that we'll be happy to reserve a jail cell for him and spend a hundred grand a year on him later," says North Carolina attorney general Mike Easley. "It's not just bad policy; it's bad arithmetic."

For some experienced offenders, the prospect of jail can make a real difference in their decisions about what crimes they are willing to commit. L.A.'s Garcetti recalls the calculating questions of a teen who raised his hand when the district attorney appeared at a detention center last April. "If I kill someone," the kid asked, "can I be executed?"

"Not at this age, no," said Garcetti.

"What if I kill more than one person?"

"Under current California law, you cannot be executed."

"Right now, I'm under 16. If I kill someone, I get out of prison when I'm 25, right?"

"Right," said Garcetti, who eventually cut off the unnerving questions by predicting, "People are so tired, so fearful and so disgusted that I think you're going to see some real changes in juvenile laws."

But few young offenders are so calculating. "These kids don't think before they do things," insists Dwayne of Atlanta, at 18 a seasoned criminal whose list of felony arrests includes armed robbery and assault. "It ain't like they stop to think, 'Now what they gonna do to me if I get caught?'" Nearby, 17-year-old DeMarcus (grand-theft auto, aggravated assault) sums up another problem: prison doesn't usually last forever, and life on the outside is an open invitation to go bad again. "They send you straight back into the same situation," he says. "The house is dirty when you left it, and it's dirty when you get back."

So the people who work with young offenders generally favor punishment for some and something like tough love for the rest. The larger problem, as always, is figuring which of the best-intended programs are better than jail cells. "Nobody has tracked the process carefully enough to find out who is good at it, in what states and by what means," says James Q. Wilson, the well-known authority on crime policy at the University of California, Los Angeles.

Knowing what works might help the Florida judge who has to decide this week on what to do about Percy Campbell. Eighteen months ago, Percy was a 12-year-old arrested for attempted burglary in northwest Fort Lauderdale. As it turned out, he already had more than 30 arrests for a total of 57 crimes on his rap sheet, some of them felonies. No surprise—he also had a mother in jail for murder and an uncle who had taught him how to steal cars.

Dennis Grant, a church elder in Fort Lauderdale, thought he could help. He gained permission to have Percy placed in the custody of his grandmother, whom Grant arranged to have relocated from a neighborhood ruled by the crack trade. The boy stayed out of trouble until June, when he broke into a neighbor's home. So it now appears that his grandmother's home wasn't the best place to be. She was arrested on shoplifting charges last week. This week a Broward County judge decides whether to try Percy as an adult or to turn him back to Grant one more time. "These kids can be changed," Grant insists. "We need to break the cycle." The prosecutors demur. "This child is being glorified," grumbles assistant state attorney Susan Aramony. "Maybe it's time to spend the resources on someone else who may benefit from them."

Percy's case highlights a key dilemma: how to distinguish kids who may be beyond change from the ones who aren't. In an article in this month's [September] *Commentary,* James Q. Wilson observes that numerous studies of young criminals tend toward a shared conclusion: in any given age group, only 6 percent of the boys will be responsible for at least half of the serious crimes committed by all boys of that age. What do those kids have in common? Criminal parents, many of them—more than half of all kids in long-term juvenile institutions in the U.S. have immediate relatives who have been incarcerated. A low verbal-intelligence quotient and poor grades are also common. The boys tend to be both emotionally cold and impulsive. From an early age they drink and get high. By an early age too, they make their first noticeable trouble, sometimes around the third grade.

If every offender who fit that profile were beyond help, judges would know better which kids to consign to lockups. They aren't all beyond help, so authorities stumble around in the dark. Indeed, the records of young offenders are generally closed, so previous offenses aren't always disclosed to judges who rule on subsequent ones. When New York State passed its juvenile-offender law in 1978, the outcome was regarded as the toughest new arrangement in the nation. On the surface, it was: those from 13 through 15 accused of heinous felonies were moved from Family Court, where the maximum penalty was 18 months regardless of the crime, to the State Supreme Court. But the law allows only for lighter sentences than would be given to adults who are convicted of equivalent crimes— meaning the kids are often back on the streets in a few years, jobless, with a felony conviction that makes employment more difficult to find.

The inadequacies of the system led Justice Michael Corriero to push for the creation of the job he now holds. He takes on all juvenile-offender cases that come through Manhattan Supreme Court. In this capacity, he has the power to fashion a midway solution for some offenders, determining whether to send convicted kids to hard time or, if he believes them salvageable, to a community-based program that keeps close tabs while offering drug counseling, job training, or schooling. Still, says Corriero, "even though the legislature gave us the bodies of these kids, they gave us no support services. We don't have a probation-department representative who tells me the Family Court history. We don't have any mental-health services to refer them to. We don't have any residential programs. We don't have any resources that the Family Court has."

Corriero wants to return all the cases to Family Court but give judges discretion to bat the worst kids back to stand trial as adults. That won't work, says Peter Reinharz, who heads the Family Court Division. It would still load too many desperate characters into a system underequipped to deal with them. "I don't know what the solution is," says Reinharz, but "I can tell you what it isn't. You're looking at it."

CALIFORNIA'S TEEN GULAGS[6]

The prisoner—call him "J"—has committed 14 serious disciplinary offenses and is confined to his cell in the lock-down unit 20 hours a day. Last week "J" attacked two guards who were escorting him back to his cell in shackles. As one guard knelt to unfasten his leg irons, "J" bolted from his cell and swung the door at the other, then hit the first guard in the head. The guards called for backup and wrestled him to the floor, then zapped him with pepper spray, a chemical agent that leaves its victim choking and in pain. Hours later, "J" was still banging on his cell door and shrieking in fury; the guard he hit went to the hospital. All this occurred at the Fred C. Nelles School in Whittier, Calif., where "J" is doing time for assault with a deadly weapon. He is 16 years old.

"J" is a prisoner in the largest juvenile-justice system in the world—the California Youth Authority, a teen gulag with nine thousand inmates in 11 training schools, including the Nelles School, and four conservation camps. CYA is the last stop for a select few of the 250,000 youth offenders arrested in California each year—the kids who commit crimes like murder, rape, and armed robbery and who, in the words of a lobbyist for the California Correctional Peace Officers Union, are "the cream of the crud."

Once famous for its innovative approaches to rehabilitation, CYA today is overcrowded, underfunded, and trapped between

[6] Article by Donna Foote from *Newsweek* Jl. 4, '94. Copyright © 1994 by Newsweek, Inc. Reprinted by permission.

society's ambivalent attitudes about juvenile crime. Rehabilitation is still a goal, and CYA officials say they're proud that 47 percent of their "graduates" stay out of the system for at least two years. But the agency's primary mission now is public safety, and that means most CYA facilities are run like adult prisons. "California violates just about anyone's standards for what to do with kids," says Barry Krisberg, president of the National Council on Crime and Delinquency. "It runs a chaotic system that is reeling out of control."

Take the Youth Training School at Chino, better known as YTS. With its tree-lined driveway and neat landscaping, YTS looks like a model youth facility. But it houses 1,672 young men between the ages of 18 and 25, almost all of whom were convicted as juveniles. About 25 percent were convicted of homicide, and many are members of street gangs like L.A.'s infamous Crips and Bloods. Although gang insignia are forbidden, YTS inmates display their gang affiliation on their necks with homemade tattoos. Fights between the gangs are commonplace, and YTS has a security squad that uses large aerosol foggers to spray pepper gas or Mace in these melees. "A lot of the kids who used to come here were right out of Father Flanagan's Boys Town," says counselor Leonard Gomez. "Now they're murderers, rapists, [and] serious drug dealers."

"It's not a pleasant place," says Adrian McCovy, 21, a model "ward" at YTS. "The majority of guys are here on gang-related crimes. If you're weak, they'll prey on you. Fights happen all the time, and at every fight [the counselors] use the gas. The particles stick to your face and you can't even open your eyes." McCovy was sent to YTS for attempted murder after two street toughs tried to steal his car—a crime he still believes was unavoidable. He is now enrolled in a college program but, like other inmates, says he has learned crime as well. "I know how to steal a car and I know how to sell drugs. I never knew how to do that before," he says. "Most guys here won't get rehabilitated. They're getting ready to go out and commit another crime."

CYA's many troubles reflect the national crime debate in miniature. Is rehabilitation still the goal, or is society now bent on keeping criminals—even very young criminals—off the streets and punishing them? CYA offers a wide variety of training programs, but funding cuts and overcrowding have made the waiting lists longer and longer. California, meanwhile, is struggling to contain a sharp increase in violent youth crime, and that means getting tough. L.A. District Attorney Gil Garcetti and other officials are pushing for a complete overhaul of the state's juvenile system, but no one knows how to balance rehabilitation with the get-tough mentality. "Rehabilitation is a nice thing to talk about," says state Assemblyman Chuck Quackenbush, author of a bill that would allow 14-year-olds to be tried as adults. "But I'm not interested in the *killer's* welfare. I'm interested in putting them in jail and protecting society. And if that means crowded prisons, so be it."

The result is a system of kiddie jails that are surrounded by razor wire, dominated by gang warfare, and regulated (if that is the word) by pepper gas—and in which some inmates are as young as 12. Is this the way to reach kids who get into trouble? And if it is, what will they be like when they get out?

II. MANDATORY SENTENCING/ VAST PRISON EXPANSION

EDITOR'S INTRODUCTION

In the 1980s Ronald Reagan inaugurated what was billed as a tougher approach to crime and criminal sentencing. Indeterminate sentences, it was argued, often allowed felons to serve minimum time and then return to the streets to commit more criminal acts. What was needed was mandatory sentencing. Fixed guideline for incarceration for specific crimes replaced the discretionary power of judges in assigning prison terms. But during the last decade, largely because of mandatory sentencing, U. S. prisons have been filled to capacity and a hugely expensive program of new prison construction is now fully underway. Yet these steps have not lowered the incidence of crime and, in the view of some, are doing more harm than good. The articles in Section Two of this volume are concerned with this controversial issue of criminal sentencing.

In the opening article reprinted from *Rolling Stone*, Neil Steinberg is critical of the inflexibly harsh sentences for drug possession meted out in federal and state courts. Steinberg asserts that in 1980 22 percent of the prison population was made up of individuals serving time for drug convictions; but in 1993 the proportion had soared to 60 percent. These people may serve more time than the most violent criminals, including even rapists and murderers.

The next article, by Jill Smolowe and reprinted from *Time*, concludes that locking up more and more people has failed as a crime deterrent. The 1980s zeal for harsh drug penalties, she asserts, has pushed the U. S. incarceration rate to 455 per 100,000 citizens, and has run up an unprecedented annual tab of $21 billion for the construction of prisons and inmate maintenance. Costs for housing prisoners run high, averaging from $23,500 per year to $74,862 per bed, in maximum security facilities, per inmate. Despite this staggering burden to taxpayers, however, the enlargement of the prison system has failed to slow the crime rate. Indeed, Smolowe maintains, it has made matters worse. In order to make room for drug offenders, the courts have been releasing violent criminals well before their sentences are served.

David C. Anderson, in a piece from the *New York Times Magazine,* rejects the "three strikes and you are out" concept embraced by President Clinton and many governors and legislators. He argues that it will have no significant impact in reducing crime because only a small percentage of the perpetrators of serious crime end up in a prison cell. To affect a larger criminal population, Anderson recommends spending money alloted to prison construction on such things as community policing, drug treatment, and an improved probation system. In a following article from *The Futurist,* Max Winkler discusses the electronic supervision programs now coming into use. Through such tracking devices as anklets and implants, low-risk criminals can be put safely on the streets instead of in prison. And, in a related piece, Jonathan Turley in an article reprinted from *USA Today* explains that prison overcrowding could be eased if elderly, low-risk prisoners were paroled.

THE LAW OF UNINTENDED CONSEQUENCES[1]

Tonya Denise Drake, a 28-year-old mother of four, mailed a package for a man she met in a parking lot, earning $47.40 and a 10-year jail sentence. Jason Cohn, 19, was sentenced to a decade in jail for shipping 12 grams of blotter paper containing LSD for a fellow Deadhead who, unknown to Cohn, had been busted by the feds. Michael Irish, a 44-year-old carpenter from Portland, Ore., spent three hours helping to unload hashish from a truck and was sentenced to 12 years in prison. Keith Edwards, 19, sold crack cocaine to a federal informant, who then set up four more buys to accumulate enough crack to qualify Edwards for the 10-year sentence he is now serving.

A decade into our nation's most recent infatuation with man-

[1] Article by Neil Steinberg from *Rolling Stone* My. 5, '94. Copyright © 1994 by Straight Arrow Publishers Company L. P. Reprinted by permission.

datory minimum sentences for drug possession, the horror stories continue to pile up. In 1993, 60 percent of the 87,000 people in federal prisons were serving time on drug convictions, up from 22 percent in 1980. Like Drake, Cohn, Irish, and Edwards, half of these prisoners were first-time offenders. Had they chosen to rob a bank or rape someone or even murder someone, their sentences would probably be less than the mandatory no-parole sentences Congress has been writing into law since 1984.

Nor are mandatory minimum sentences limited to the federal government. Forty-nine states have their own mandatory laws, such as Michigan's "650 Lifer" law, which requires life sentences for possession of more than 650 grams of cocaine. In that state, some 150 people are sitting in prison for life for cocaine possession, perhaps half of them first offenders like Gary Fannon Jr., now 25 and seven years into the life sentence he got for a drug transaction that he merely helped to arrange.

Compulsory drug sentencing is kept alive by fearmongering. After creating the first set of harsh mandatory-drug-sentencing laws, the infamous Boggs Act, in the 1950s, then repealing them as unworkable in 1970, Congress plunged back into mandatory minimums with the Comprehensive Crime Control Act of 1984. Since then, stiffening or adding to the mandatory minimums has been an election-year ritual, with the Anti-Drug Abuse Acts of 1986 and 1988 and the 1990 crime bill. The 1992 crime bill died at the end of the congressional session only because of the gun-control controversy.

New to her job, Attorney General Janet Reno appeared to have taken a position on mandatory minimums based on common sense and experience. Unwisely, she spoke up: "We are not going to solve the crime problem by sending everyone to prison for as long as we can get them there and throwing away the key." Apparently chastened by the administration, she has backed off. Her office now insists: "Attorney General Reno never was against mandatory minimum sentences. She said we need to look at them and determine who they're affecting. She is still saying the same exact thing."

President Clinton declined an invitation to talk to *Rolling Stone* on mandatory minimums, and members of the Senate and House judiciary committees, fearful of being called soft on crime, tend to be reluctant to discuss the subject publicly. Of 10 key members polled for their opinion for this article, only Orrin Hatch, the ranking member of the Senate Judiciary Committee, responded.

"He's recognized the problem of inflexibility when dealing with drug cases," a spokesman said. "He's willing to try to give the judges some measure of flexibility. The problem is, people can't agree on a definition."

The original purpose of mandatory minimums was to eliminate discrepancies between the sentences given for the same drug crimes in more liberal and more conservative areas of the nation. But in guaranteeing that liberal regions punish criminals adequately, Congress couldn't resist the opportunity to proclaim its moral indignation. So it created particularly punitive mandatory sentences—five years in prison for possession of a gram of LSD or five grams of cocaine, 10 years in prison for growing 1,000 marijuana plants or selling a kilogram of heroin.

Most would agree a kilo is a lot of heroin, and the guy who peddles it in a schoolyard should probably go to prison for a decade. But in real life, the situation is seldom so clear. Under the law, the guy who sells the heroin to schoolchildren and the buddy who watches out for the police are guilty of the same crime. The girlfriend who gives a DEA informant the boyfriend's phone number and the mook who lets the kilo sit in his locker overnight for $10 are also guilty of the same crime. Whereas previously a judge might vary their sentences to reflect varying degrees of culpability, under mandatory minimums, that latitude no longer exists, and federal judges are incensed about it.

"Without any elbow room, you cripple the whole system," says Judge William J. Bauer of the U.S. Court of Appeals for the 7th Circuit. Milton Shadur, senior U.S. district judge in Illinois, concurs: "In a word, mandatory minimum sentences, as they operate in the federal system, particularly in drug cases, are a disaster."

At least one federal judge, J. Lawrence Irving, resigned from the bench rather than impose the sentences. "It's insanity," says Irving, now a private mediator. "We're putting young people in prison for 10 years on their first offense without possibility of parole, a longer sentence than is served in many states for murder. . . . I couldn't in good conscience impose sentences I felt were draconian."

Despite growing opposition, mandatory minimums have cast a widening net. In 1984, 10 percent of federal defendants were subject to mandatory minimum sentences; by 1990, 20 percent were.

The single loophole judges can use to impose a sentence lower than the mandatory one is cooperation. Prosecutors praise this as a tool for cracking the most tight-lipped felons. But in real life, it rewards people for higher levels of involvement in the drug trade. The former hippie with 1,000 marijuana plants growing in his basement and no drug ring to rat on gets the full decade in prison, while the savvy dealer bringing in boatloads of pot from south of the border can finger a few friends and be out in half the time.

Supporters of mandatory sentencing tend to look at the big picture. "The only way to get a real hammer effect on some crimes is to set a floor below which the judge cannot go," former attorney general William P. Barr has said. "The drug problem is a national scourge."

The most comprehensive indictment of mandatory minimums comes from the U.S. Sentencing Commission, which, at the request of Congress, issued a lengthy study on the subject in August 1991. Calling the sentences "single-shot efforts at crime control intended to produce dramatic results," the commission found a host of major flaws in the system:

• Mandatory minimums fail to make sentencing more uniform, because the sentences are not applied uniformly. More than a third of the defendants subject to mandatory sentences plea-bargain instead. Thus disparities are not eliminated. Rather, discretion is shifted from judges, who exercise it publicly from the bench, to prosecutors, who exercise it secretly. As Judge Terry J. Hatter Jr. of the Central District of California puts it: "I, as a sitting lifetime judge appointed by the president and confirmed by the Senate, have less authority now than 30 years ago, when I was an assistant U.S. attorney."

• Mandatory minimums are invoked more often with black defendants than white ones. Blacks make up 28.2 percent of the federal prison population but 38.5 percent of mandatory-minimum defendants.

• While sentencing guidelines seek "a smooth continuum," mandatory minimums result in "cliffs," or major differences in the sentence based on tiny changes in the crime. For example, the difference of one milligram of crack cocaine can change the sentence from a maximum of one year in prison to a minimum of five years.

• Consideration of prior records is broad and often bizarre in federal cases. "A single prior conviction for a felony drug offense doubles the mandatory minimum sentence," the commission wrote. "It is the same whether the conviction occurred 20 years ago or a month ago; it is the same if the prior conviction occurred in state court for the same conduct."

All sorts of strange provisions are included in mandatory-minimum bills. The Senate's pending crime bill would double the penalty for selling drugs if the sale occurs within 1,000 feet of a truck stop or rest area. The 1988 crime bill included a provision that made the amount of crack cocaine needed to trigger a mandatory sentence one hundred times less than its powdered variant. The intent was to address crack's impact on the inner city, but the effect has been to divide mandatory sentences along racial lines: Blacks make up 90 percent of the defendants in crack cases but only 25 percent in the less harshly punished powder-cocaine cases. A federal judge—Lyle E. Strom of Omaha, Neb.—ruled in one case that blacks convicted in crack cases "are being treated unfairly in receiving substantially longer sentences than caucasian males, who traditionally deal in powder cocaine."

The good news, if it is not premature to call it that, is that some members of Congress have begun to try to undo the damage. Last month, Rep. Charles Schumer, D-N.Y., working with Rep. Henry Hyde, R-Ill., managed to get the House Judiciary Committee to approve a "safety valve" provision. It would permit a judge to drop the mandatory five-year sentence for simple drug possession to two years—if the offender wasn't violent, didn't use a gun, and had not been sent to prison previously for more than 60 days.

The safety-valve provision would be retroactive. That aspect of the proposal drew the most complaints from the Justice Department, which expressed concern that freeing prisoners serving excessively harsh sentences would clog the courts and create paperwork. Several members of Congress expressed astonishment at the Justice Department's position. "The notion that this might inconvenience the Justice Department is distressing," said Rep. Barney Frank of Massachusetts.

There is also hope for action on the state levels. Even in Michigan, legislators were holding hearings last month on adding safety valves to the 650 Lifer law to give nonviolent first-time offenders such as Gary Fannon a way out.

"There's a lot of good things happening right now," says Fannon, who was transferred in October to the medium-security prison in Coldwater. "A lot of big names are involved: the Michigan attorney general, some federal judges, and state judges. The 650 Lifer law could be amended to give the judge discretion to impose life with parole when dealing with first-time nonviolent offenders who don't have any high misdemeanors."

But any hope for change remains just that—hope. The Senate crime bill is still packed with all sorts of new punishments, such as mandatory life sentences for a second conviction of selling drugs to a minor or for any three drug convictions. Sen. Bob Dole of Kansas is also trying to smash the gang problem by creating whole new categories of federal crimes and mandatory sentences to fit them, from persuading someone to join a gang (five years) to belonging to a gang that commits murder (life). The Dole proposals could have staggering implications—hundreds of people could be jailed for life based on the commission of a single crime by a fellow gang member.

To deal with the flood of new prisoners, the Senate bill sets aside billions for the construction of more prisons and voids all previous court-ordered prison-population caps. So not only would more drug offenders be dropped into prison for longer periods of time, but those prisons would be crowded beyond what was once considered the point of inhumanity.

It may be the cost of the crime bill—each new cell could cost up to $100,000—that helps bring an end to Congress' infatuation with mandatory minimums. "The economics of the thing can't be avoided," says Adam Kurland, a law professor at Howard University, in Washington, D.C., and also a former assistant U.S. attorney. "When the taxpayers realize they have no money for schools and all they're doing is building more prisons, it encourages people to resist mandatory minimums and their consequences."

. . . AND THROW AWAY THE KEY[2]

For years, Tonya Drake struggled from one welfare check to the next, juggling the cost of diapers, food, and housing for her four small children, all under age eight. So when Drake, 30, was handed a $100 bill by a man she barely knew in June 1990 and was told she could keep the change if she posted a package for him, she readily agreed. For her effort, Drake received $47.70

    [2] Article by Jill Smolowe from *Time* F. 7, '94. Copyright © 1994 by Time Inc. Reprinted by permission.

and assumed that would be the end of it. But unknown to Drake, the package contained 232 grams of crack cocaine. Although she had neither a prior criminal record nor any history of drug use, the judge was forced under federal mandatory-sentencing guidelines to impose a 10-year prison term. At the sentencing, District Judge Richard Gadbois Jr. lamented, "That's just crazy, but there's nothing I can do about it."

Now, while Drake serves her time in a federal prison in Dublin, California, at a cost to taxpayers of about $25,000 a year, her children must live with her family 320 miles south in Inglewood. "How are you going to teach her a lesson by sending her to prison for 10 years?" demands her attorney, Robert Campbell III. "What danger is she to society?" Penologists have a ready answer: the danger is that while Drake monopolizes a scarce federal-prison bed, she enables a more dangerous criminal to roam free. To them, Drake's case is a textbook example of the myopia that blinds Americans to the long-term consequences of short-term solutions.

The disturbing truth is that although three decades of lock-'em-up fever have made America the world's No. 1 jailer, there still aren't nearly enough cells to go around. The '80s zeal for harsh drug penalties has pushed the U.S. incarceration rate to 455 per 100,000 citizens and has run up an unprecedented annual tab of $21 billion for the construction of prisons and maintenance of inmates. As the nation's inmate population swells toward 1.4 million, prison officials must release career criminals to make room for first-time drug offenders. The growing public outcry against violent crime is prompting politicians to call for even stiffer, tighter, and costlier sanctions. But more prisons and longer sentences likely point in only two directions: larger inmate rosters and a higher crime rate. Robert Gangi, executive director of the Correctional Association of New York, warns, "Building more prisons to address crime is like building more graveyards to address a fatal disease."

Americans' impatience for quick-fix remedies resembles the frustration that drives inner-city youths to seize on illegal get-rich schemes: they want to cut corners, produce high yields, and not pay a price. But grim experience indicates that, as with crime, hard time doesn't always pay the anticipated dividends. When money is poured into building another prison cell at the expense of rebuilding a prisoner's self-image, it is often just a prelude to more—and worse—crime. "They start as drug offenders, they eventually become property-crime offenders, and then they commit crimes against people," says Michael Sheahan, the sheriff of Cook County, Illinois. "They learn this trade as they go through the prison system."

America has already been trying to jail its way out of the crime problem—with discouraging results. Over the past two decades, the U.S. has hosted the biggest prison-construction boom in history, laying out $37 billion, with $5 billion more in the pipeline. Yet the pool of street criminals keeps rising. In the past decade, the number of federal and state inmates has doubled, to 925,000, while the local jail population has nearly tripled, to 450,000. State by state, the outlook is bleak. Washington, for instance, has witnessed a 79 percent increase in its jail population and an 86 percent increase in prison capacity, though the state population has grown just 18 percent. "At that rate," says Governor Mike Lowry, "everyone in Washington State will be working in—or in—prison by 2056."

The prison buildup has not come cheaply. The average annual cost per inmate is now $23,500. The average cost per bed in maximum-security facilities is $74,862. "You don't lock them up and throw away the key," says Howard Peters, Illinois' director of corrections. "You lock them up and spend thousands of dollars on them."

But to what end? The politically popular war on drugs of the '80s has given rise to the far less sexy cell crunch of the '90s. Mandatory minimum sentences for minor drug crimes have stuffed the prisons to bursting with nonviolent offenders. By 1990 almost 40 states were under court order to relieve overcrowding by releasing prisoners—even habitual offenders. Today narcotics offenders occupy 61 percent of the beds in federal prisons. Meanwhile, one in seven state facilities continues to operate beyond capacity. Ohio leads the pack with a stunning 182 percent of capacity.

Such pressures require creative reshuffling. In North Carolina, where a net gain of 200 new inmates each week has made a mockery of the statutory limit of 21,400, Governor James Hunt Jr. will present a new crime-fighting package to the legislature next week. His proposals include rushing the opening of two of the 12 new prisons currently under construction and leasing space in county jails. Meanwhile, North Carolina is trying to ship one thousand inmates over state lines. To date, Oklahoma and Rhode Island have contracted to house temporarily a total of 226 inmates. Even so, unless Hunt can persuade legislators to raise the statutory cap by March 15, he will be forced to release 3,400 inmates.

And therein lies the rub. The mandatory sentences that keep drug offenders in push violent criminals out. In Florida drug sentences of, on average, four years have cut time dramatically for other inmates. The average prisoner serves just 41 percent of his time; serious thugs do half. Although the standard sentence for robbery is 8.6 years and almost 22 years for murder, the average prison stay is just 16 months. Harry Singletary, who heads the state's department of corrections, dryly calls himself the "Secretary of Release." He might just as well call himself the "Secretary of Readmission." Since 1991, some 43,000 convicts who were released early because of overcrowding have been rearrested. That makes for a recidivism rate of 34 percent, well in line with the national average of 35 percent.

That disheartening statistic applies only to those who actually go to prison. Overcrowding has enabled countless more repeat offenders to elude incarceration or do snooze time in a county jail. According to Marc Mauer of the Washington-based Sentencing Project, for each crime committed, an offender stands a one-in-20 chance of serving time. "People ignore the gun laws because there are no stiff penalties," says Antoine McClarn, 22, who sits in the Cook County Jail on charges of armed robbery. "Guys are charged and then released, and it's like a cycle to them, almost fun. People used to be scared to come here, but now it's a game or a joke."

The upshot is that while jails and prisons still incapacitate, incarcerate, and punish, they no longer—if they ever did—deter crime. Indeed, in many inner-city neighborhoods, young men regard prison time as more a rite of passage than a deterrent. "Their father's been in prison, their brother's been in prison," says Lieut. Robert Losack, 30, who has served as a Texas prison guard for nine years. "It's socially acceptable; it's part of growing up." Once back on the street, these youths enjoy an enhanced status. They also pose a greater threat. "Prison culture becomes the model for street society," warns Jerome Miller, president of the National Center on Institutions and Alternatives in Washington. "Young black men take onto the streets the ethics, morals, and rules of the maximum-security prison."

Or they return with new wiles learned in local cells. Until he turned his life around 18 months ago in a drug-rehabilitation program, Lorenzo Woodley, 35, spent most of his time getting into—and out of—jail. Since age 19, Woodley has been arrested 14 times, all on felonies ranging from burglary to selling cocaine. Yet the longest stretch he ever spent locked up was six months in Miami's Dade County Jail. He has yet to see the inside of a prison. "I was a very manipulative person," he says with a smile. "You tell a judge you got a drug problem. Judges get soft. They know what drugs do to people. They send you to a drug-rehab program instead of prison." Jail suited Woodley just fine. "You get healthy, you sleep good, you eat good, you get cable TV." Then you get out. "They don't rehab you at all. They don't teach you anything," he says. "So these guys come out and do the same thing all over again."

That revolving door helps explain why 80 percent of all crimes are committed by about 20 percent of the criminals. It also helps to make sense of the seeming contradiction that many states with high incarceration rates also have high violent crime rates. Florida has the twelfth highest lock-up rate among states, and it ranks first in violent crime. Conversely, 12 of the 15 states with the lowest incarceration rates also score low on violent crime. Minnesota, for instance, has the nation's second lowest incarceration rate, jailing just 90 people per one hundred thousand, and is ranked 37th for violent crime. It is probably no coincidence that Minnesota is one of the most progressive states on punishment. Prisoners who are functionally illiterate—35 percent of the inmates—must take a reading course before they can join other classes. Some 90 percent of those inmates have enrolled.

Such results have convinced people who spend most of their waking hours in and around prisons—commissioners, wardens, guards, not to mention inmates—that if prisons only punish, and offer no inducements or opportunities for rehabilitation, they simply produce tougher criminals. When prisoners have no constructive way to spend their time, they often fill the hours building a reservoir of resentment, not to mention a grab bag of criminal tricks, that—count on it—they will take back to the streets. "All we do," says Dr. John May, one of the 10 doctors who service the nine thousand inmates at Chicago's Cook County Jail, "is produce someone meaner and angrier and more disillusioned with himself and society."

A minority counters that prisons serve a valuable function beyond safeguarding citizens from criminals. "How can you say [prisons] have no impact on crime rates?" challenges Charlie Parsons, who heads the FBI's Los Angeles Regional Office. He points to an FBI effort to curb bank robberies that slashed such incidents in Southern California by 37 percent in a year. "The bottom line is that if you catch somebody after their first bank robbery or after their tenth, you are going to have an impact," he says. Director Peters of Illinois also sees benefit in stiff time. "For many of the inmates, prison is the first time they have ever had order in their lives," he says. "The average inmate leaves prison either the same or a little better than when he came in."

The far more prevalent view, though, is that the revolving door puts seasoned criminals back onto the streets to make room for nonviolent offenders, who make up half the prison population. "Prison systems are 'criminogenic': they create criminals," says University of Miami criminologist Paul Cromwell, who served as a commissioner on the Texas Board of Pardons and Paroles. The chronic beatings, stabbings, rapes, and isolation ignite fury. "Just about everyone I talk to says that when they get out they will do something bad," says Larry Jobe, 32, who is imprisoned at a supermax facility in Oak Park Heights, Minnesota. "They are so blind with rage that they can't think about the consequences." Jobe, a former accountant who is serving life for a murder he insists he did not commit, knows the risk of long sentences: "After so many years, they have nothing to lose."

Even the softest inmates can turn into violent thugs. There is no telling yet if Randy Blackburn, 31, will become such a person, but he is worried he might. Blackburn has been in Cook County Jail for the past 13 months, awaiting trial on sexual assault. "I almost felt like a baby," he says of his first days in lockup. "I really didn't know what cocaine was until I got here." Now, Blackburn says, the temptation to become "hard" is constant. "Every night in the dorm, you hear the guys talk about how many people they have shot and how much drugs they've sold and women they've had. It can lead you into that."

Sheer boredom also stokes the rage. Jails, which are designed for short-term incarceration, provide few educational or work opportunities. Prisons do better. Most offer some courses, though tight budgets have forced cutbacks in recent years; two out of three prison inmates have work assignments. Even so, a quarter of all prisoners have neither jobs nor classes to engage their time and pent-up energies.

Corrections officials know there are no quick fixes. But they—like many inmates—argue that the prison system would function more effectively if justice were served more swiftly, sentences imposed more reliably, and space allocated more rationally. The lag of months, sometimes years, between the crime and the punishment is counterproductive. Says Marcus Felson, a sociology professor at the University of Southern California: "[An electric] plug that shocks you a year later or once in a thousand times isn't going to deter you."

Neither are sentences that telescope years into months. "That six months I served, that was a slap on the wrist," says Woodley, who turned himself around without going to prison. "If you get three years, you should do three years." At the same time, the jailers know that prisoners need incentives for good behavior. Florida's Singletary favors 75 percent sentences for those of the 53,000 prisoners in his system who "work off" days by doing construction work, cleaning parks, and performing other outside tasks. It not only lessens tension within the prison but also addresses the problem of idleness.

Work programs can benefit inmates and taxpayers alike. Minnesota's Sentencing to Service program has been putting nonviolent offenders to work in communities throughout the state since 1986. So far, it has logged 530,000 man-hours, and when program costs are offset against earnings and reductions in prison costs, the effort comes up $6 million in the black. "In work programs, inmates feel like they're paying back society," says Charles Colson, who established the Prison Fellowship after serving seven highly publicized months in prison. "Work restores their sense of dignity—and it's useful to society."

Precious prison space must also be allocated more judiciously. Penologists say that means not only finding alternative penalties for nonviolent offenders, but offering parole to rehabilitated old-timers. Often the hotheads who enter the system while still in their teens and 20s chill out by their 30s and 40s. Life-means-life sentences do a disservice on several fronts. Taxpayers pay ever steeper costs for aging inmates, who require more medical care; wardens are stripped of the ability to motivate these prisoners; and the lifers sink into a hopelessness that can be dangerous.

Most important, the problems connected with crime—inadequate schooling, unemployment, drugs, unstable families—must be addressed as part of America's prison crisis. "Look, I'm not a bleeding-heart liberal; I'm a realist," says Singletary. "But the cure for our crime is *not* prison beds and juvenile boot camps.

We need to do something about juveniles at the school level before they get here."

President Clinton sounded the same alarm last week in his State of the Union Address. "I ask you to remember that even as we say no to crime, we must give people, especially our young people, something to say yes to." The question is whether America was listening.

'LOCK 'EM UP' CAN'T POSSIBLY CUT CRIME MUCH[3]

People in California will not soon forget Polly Klaas and Kimber Reynolds.

A man abducted 12-year-old Polly from a slumber party in her own house, as her mother slept. He drove her away, strangled her, and dumped her body at an abandoned lumber mill. Kimber, 18, was leaving a restaurant with a friend when two men on motorcycles roared up beside them. One grabbed her purse, and when she struggled he shot her in the head.

The men arrested for these murders turned out to have had long criminal records, and Polly and Kimber came to symbolize a specific response to public fury: life in prison for repeat offenders, or three strikes and you're out. The idea has swept the country and has been embraced by President Clinton, members of Congress, governors and legislators of several states. To most Americans, it seems like common sense: keeping dangerous criminals in prison longer will reduce crime and make life safer.

But does it make sense? However horrifying the individual cases may be, the use of sentencing laws to control crime can never have more than a marginal effect. The reason is clear from the arithmetic of criminal justice.

The numbers, published regularly by Federal agencies, constitute a big funnel. The 35 million crimes committed each year pour in at the top—everything from shoplifting, auto theft, and drunken fights to rapes and murders. Of these, about 25 million are serious, since they involve violence or sizable property loss.

[3] Article by David C. Anderson from the *New York Times Magazine* Je. 12, '94. Copyright © 1994 by the New York Times Company. Reprinted by permission.

But millions of these crimes go unpunished because the victims never report them. Only 15 million serious crimes come to the attention of the police.

The disparity between crimes suffered and crimes reported was a stunning revelation in the 1970's, after the Census Bureau began polling the general public to come up with estimates of crimes committed. Year after year, the number of crimes people said they had experienced far exceeded the crimes they reported to the police.

A subsequent survey for the National Institute of Justice explained the discrepancy. Victims told researchers they didn't consider the crimes important enough to report or they involved matters to settle privately. Many saw little chance the culprits would be arrested or lost property recovered, so why hassle with the cops?

That's the first narrowing of the funnel. The next comes at the point of apprehension. Each year, the police make arrests in only 21 percent of the 15 million most serious crimes—homicides, rapes, robberies, aggravated assaults, burglaries, larcenies, and auto thefts. As a result, 3.2 million criminals are turned over to the courts for prosecution.

Why does only one serious reported crime out of five lead to an arrest? In millions of cases, arrests are made but disposed of as misdemeanors. Hundreds of thousands of other cases are turned over to the juvenile-justice system. In many urban neighborhoods, the police are simply overwhelmed by the volume of crime and can't hope to investigate each case aggressively. Millions of burglaries and auto thefts are reported for insurance purposes— not because anyone expects the police to make an arrest.

Further winnowing takes place in courthouses, as cases are dismissed for lack of evidence, because witnesses disappear or refuse to cooperate, or for other technical reasons. Of the 3.2 million criminals arrested, 81 percent are actually prosecuted; prosecutors obtain convictions of 59 percent, or 1.9 million.

Now their fate is up to judges, who follow sentencing laws that vary considerably from state to state. Nearly everywhere, judges consider prison space a precious commodity to be used only when it makes obvious sense. Younger criminals convicted of their first or second offenses commonly get off with probation or suspended sentences. In the end, about 500,000 of the 1.9 million convicts are sent behind bars, a trickle from the funnel's stem compared with the flood of 35 million at its mouth.

The process that reduces flood to trickle costs taxpayers some $74 billion annually. The part that has changed most dramatically over the years is the number of people actually locked up. In 1980, the figure was about two hundred thousand. During the next decade, states and the Federal Government embarked on a historic prison expansion binge. They spent more than $90 billion to triple the total amount of prison space. That boosted the annual operating cost to about $25 billion—a third of all the money spent to deal with crime.

Americans may think that the crime rate is worse than ever, but it actually fell somewhat during the 1980's. Violent offenses per one thousand people declined from 33.3 in 1980 to 31.3 in 1991. Was that because of the big prison buildup? That's hard to believe, considering the difference in magnitude between a few hundred thousand criminals and tens of millions of crimes. Even after the prison buildup, only 1.4 percent of crimes result in imprisonment, only 2 percent of serious crimes. More likely, crime has fallen because of change in the structure of the population. During the 1980's, the number of young people—who commit the most crimes—declined as the median age of Americans rose from 30 to 33.

Even so, when frustrated, fearful Americans hear about Polly Klaas and Kimber Reynolds, they like the sound of prison as a way to give criminals what they deserve. Tough sentencing sounds like strong medicine, even if its effects are often illusory.

Three strikes and you're out? In truth, such a law will probably have no more than a slight effect on public safety. For one thing, the plea bargaining that dominates criminal justice eats deeply into the certainty the law seems to promise. And even if it should be widely applied, a three-strikes law offers no hope for immediate relief. It could not be applied retroactively to the existing population of convicted felons sentenced to terms far shorter than life and likely to be paroled over the next several years.

Still, state legislators and members of Congress, reactive as ever, are desperate to appease public fear and outrage. They have little patience with troublesome facts and reach for comforting illusions. But to what end?

Suppose the current political mood generates a new round of sentencing laws tough enough to boost the number locked up each year to more than one million. That might cost taxpayers about $150 billion over a decade, or $15 billion a year. But it is very unlikely that an expansion of that magnitude would be enough to change the shape of the crime funnel. Even if crime continued its gradual decline to, say, 30 million a year, the new prison construction would raise the number incarcerated to only about 3 percent of the number of offenses.

These numbers are often seized upon by old liberals who never liked the idea of building prisons. Why pour more money into steel and concrete that don't do much for crime control, they say, when schools, health care, and other social programs go begging? Yet politicians know that the public wants a more direct response to crime. For now, three strikes looks as good as any. And that is where the discussion usually ends.

But take another look at the funnel. Its sharply angled shape raises an obvious question: Why just tinker with the stem? Why not see what might be done at earlier levels of the process? For the sake of argument, consider different ways to spend the $15 billion a year now likely to be spent on new prisons. It could, for instance, be divided among three practical measures that are widely accepted as sound ways to reduce crime:

Spend $5 Billion to Hire More Officers for Community Policing.

Most police work is reactive—responding to calls for help. Not surprisingly, that hardly serves as a deterrent to criminals. Studies show remarkably little connection between levels of crime and levels of traditional police activity. So why spend money for more cops?

Community policing provides an answer. Gaining popularity with police managers across America, this approach sends officers out to work together with communities to attack crime problems. Are landlords profiteering, for example, by renting to drug dealers? Dispatching cops to arrest the dealers, the traditional response, doesn't work. More dealers quickly move in. To get landlords to evict the dealers and to stop renting to other dealers, community police might help the neighbors challenge the landlords in court, or lodge complaints with a city housing agency or fire department, or even picket the landlords' homes in the suburbs.

Many communities attest to the success of this approach. But implementing it well requires more officers than most departments have to spare. The police still must respond to 911 calls even as they do more creative work with neighborhoods. And some tradition-bound cops resist the idea. But a big infusion of

Federal money—$5 billion would pay for 100,000 police—might change that in a hurry.

Spend $5 Billion on Drug Treatment.

Surveys of people arrested show phenomenal rates of drug use. In 1990, more than 66 percent of men charged with robbery and 68 percent of those charged with burglary tested positive for drugs. Those who undergo treatment and recover from their addictions are likely to commit fewer crimes. The long-term prognosis for them is better than for those who spend a few years in prison without drug treatment.

Americans have known for years how to treat drug addiction effectively. Yet addicts seeking treatment are often put on waiting lists. A 1989 study found that 79,072 people appeared on such lists nationwide. That figure understates the unmet demand, since treatment programs rarely market their services.

Five billion dollars would pay for about two million new treatment slots a year, nearly quadrupling the existing capacity. With the number of people needing treatment now estimated at three to four times the number receiving it, that could make a dent in the problem. Expanded capacity might also give more judges the option of sentencing drug-related offenders to treatment programs, on pain of imprisonment if they fail to participate.

Invest $5 Billion to Improve Probation.

There are more than twice as many convicts on probation—released to the community under court supervision—as in prison. Yet for the majority, supervision is a joke. Probation departments are so understaffed that a probation officer may have more than one hundred cases at a time. A few states and cities have spent money to reduce individual caseloads to 25 or so and establish a number of "intermediate sanctions"—electronic monitoring, drug testing and treatment, boot camps—that combine social services with various levels of control. The concept permits courts to intervene at an early stage with younger offenders, creating the real possibility, now all but nonexistent, that criminal justice could actually turn their lives around.

Community police, drug treatment, and probation are not the only possibilities. Some of the $15 billion might be invested in continued research and evaluation of other crime reduction mea-

sures. But there is no arguing with the basic shape of the crime
funnel—or the idea that a shift in emphasis from bottom to top
would gain much and risk losing very little. The point of such a
strategy would be to stop crimes by the million, rather than lock
up criminals by the thousand—to shrink the mouth of the funnel
instead of spending mindlessly to slightly widen its stem.

WALKING PRISONS[4]

The cost of incarcerating criminals in America has steadily
spiraled upward. Maximum-security incarceration now requires
an average of $25,000 per year per inmate, with an initial cost of
$100,000 to construct a one-inmate cell. The costs of local deten-
tion and jail units are also on the rise, now averaging $18,000 per
year per inmate. Such massive costs provide a compelling reason
to shorten prison terms or to reserve incarceration for the most
dangerous and threatening of criminals.

Alternatives to imprisonment are increasingly being offered,
but humanitarianism alone is not enough to justify releasing prisoners for good behavior, conferring leniency on first-time offenders, or offering work-release or other such programs where
the offender is supervised in the community.

One revolutionary alternative for controlling criminals is a
system known as the Electronic Supervision Program. It may
prove a precursor of felon-supervision systems in the new millen-
nium. The Electronic Supervision Program is now a popular system for managing offenders by means of electronic monitors.
The system enables law-enforcement agents to keep better track
of inmates released from prison.

Drive-By Tracking

The Electronic Supervision Program's home-detention system is based on current technology available from a variety of
national and international corporations. This first-generation
system consists of an anklet transponder electronically linked to a
telephone modem. Its purpose is to alert a central monitoring

[4] Article by Max Winkler from *The Futurist* Jl./Ag. '93. Copyright © 1993 by
The Futurist, Bethesda, Maryland. Reprinted by permission.

station when the offender moves outside of a 100-foot radius around the modem. The system also periodically checks the offender's location. Attempts to leave the specified location or to tamper with the transponder are relayed back to the monitoring station automatically.

The system also allows law-enforcement officers with "drive-by" units to check on offenders at their workplace, home, or other authorized locations. The officer's car has a portable electronic receiver that displays the frequency code of the nearest transponder unit. Often, drive-by units get signals from unexpected locations, such as city jails or locations with reported crimes in progress.

At present, the system offers a multitude of applications. Recently, an offender in Colorado with a propensity for violence (and an old grudge toward the parole officers who revoked his parole) was fitted with one of these anklet transponders. The parole officers carried a portable drive-by unit, which would have sounded an alarm if the offender had either followed the officers' car or gotten within 200 feet of their homes.

Stores and other businesses with hidden frequency detectors at their entrances could also make use of this technology. The arrival of an ankleted shoplifter would set off a silent alarm, and the system would identify the offender to the store management.

One further advantage of this electronic system is its low cost: an average of only $8 per day, which would be paid for by the offender.

Counting Blips

A second-generation monitoring system consisting of computer-controlled radio receivers will likely be in place between 1995 and 2000. This system will instantly record every place the offender goes—not just when he or she is out of the range of the home-detention modem.

An anklet (or bracelet) transponder would send out a blip signal every five to 10 seconds that would be picked up by two separate receivers. The arrival times of the blips would determine the offender's approximate location on a city or regional grid map. The signal would also include a unique frequency code to identify whose transponder was "blipping." (This system could also be adapted to use cellular phone transmitters, providing even greater accuracy in determining an offender's location.)

Every place the offender went—and the time he or she was

there—would be recorded and compiled and could then be cross-indexed against known crime scenes and times. A location and time matching a person on this system would be sufficient for a probable-cause detention, if not clear evidence of a new crime. It is also feasible for the system to set off an alarm when an offender approaches a location that is either restricted or forbidden, such as the home of a former victim or an estranged spouse with a restraining order. Offenders can also be restricted to specific locations and routes in a city, with any divergences or breaches immediately noted.

The weak link, literally speaking, is the anklet or bracelet transponder itself. The attaching device will certainly have to be made more secure and tamperproof. The use of steel or fiber-composite reinforcement in the band could prevent or significantly delay tampering. It should also be fairly basic to set up a program to send out an alarm and location signal when tampering begins.

The immediate benefits of a radio (or cellular) locater system can be dramatic. Low-risk offenders could be released to the streets en masse and strictly supervised at a cost that they themselves are likely to pay for. Coordination between street-level law-enforcement officers and parole and probation personnel would have to be markedly increased. But with this system in place, officers could be notified of a crime being committed, or even likely to be committed, almost instantaneously.

The end of the 1990s will likely see a hugely improved system of parolee and probationer supervision at a greatly reduced cost. If the system succeeds, the public may support the release of nonviolent, low-risk offenders from costly correctional facilities, leaving only the violent, high-risk criminals behind bars.

Fuzzy Logic Chips and Shut-Down Implants

The third generation of electronic supervision incorporating radio monitors, fuzzy logic, and medical implants will likely be in place sometime after 2001. Custom-programmed microprocessor chips would monitor the offender's physiological patterns and reactions and would recognize the advent of a violent or severely aberrant phase. The microprocessor could then send out an alarm to the nearest receiver, which would relay it to the central monitoring station.

It may be feasible to implant the monitor under the skin,

radically reducing attempts at tampering. Such systems could be used to control the offender's behavior if it were combined with a tiny reservoir of drugs that could be injected into the bloodstream. The unit containing the drugs would also be implanted under the skin, as with the Norplant® contraceptive. When unsuitable or alarming behavior is indicated, the microprocessor could trigger the release of a measured amount of tranquilizer or a sexually dampening chemical. For example, a sex offender's specific patterns of aberrant sexuality would be recognized by the programmed chip, and the drugs would selectively tone down criminally sanctioned behaviors but allow normal or acceptable sexuality.

There may also be the option to "shut down" an offender by the use of sleep-inducing chemicals. Such a third-generation system could allow even maximum-security offenders to be released relatively safely into society. While such a monitoring and control system risks the danger of exploitation and could conceivably contribute to the ultimate totalitarian society, it offers great benefits and can enlarge people's freedom. Convicted offenders would have the chance to participate productively in a free society. Average citizens would be more secure, free from victimization, and less taxed to pay for prisons.

A SOLUTION TO PRISON OVERCROWDING[5]

On June 7, 1973, Quenton Brown, a 50-year-old homeless man, walked into a small bread store in rural Louisiana and stole $100 and a 15-cent pie. While a number of people watched, Brown left the store and crawled under a house across the street, where he remained until the police arrived. After his arrest, the state found Brown had a 51 I.Q.—the intelligence level of a three-and-one-half-year-old child. After a one-day trial, he was given a 30-year sentence without chance of parole for armed robbery. Now 69 years old, Brown has been at Angola State Penitentiary for 19 years.

[5] Article by Johnathan Turley from *USA Today* N. '92. Copyright © 1992 by USA Today. Reprinted by permission.

Brown is an example of an emerging national scandal—the failure of the prison system to release geriatric low-risk prisoners to make room for younger, more dangerous ones. At a time when our correctional facilities literally are turning away hundreds of drug dealers because of overcrowding, they continue to hold prohibition-era felons. The number of elderly in the state and Federal prisons has doubled in the last four years. By 2001, there will be more than 125,000 older prisoners in this country.

The maintenance costs alone for these inmates are staggering. Geriatric services are exceptionally expensive in facilities that are built for incarceration, not convalescence. An elderly prisoner will undergo an average of three chronic illnesses during his or her incarceration. Brown, for example, suffers from a crushed esophagus and double ulcers. The average health cost of an elderly individual is $69,000—three times that for younger inmates. This does not include expensive alterations that must be made to accommodate elderly prisoners, including replacing uniform buttons with velcro patches; expansion of doors and the addition of ramps to allow for wheelchairs; and specialized diets.

Many of those in both the state and Federal systems are completely bedridden or require extraordinary medical attention. I met many of these prisoners on trips to Louisiana, Maryland, and other states, such as Harvey Edwards, a 59-year-old child molester, who needed two shots of insulin and 32 pills per day for high blood pressure and a heart condition. Half-blind and paralyzed on his right side, he required a walker to move around.

William Hankins, a 62-year-old convicted murderer, was driven to Baton Rouge three times a week for treatment on a dialysis machine, on which he has spent more than 23,000 hours. In a state that spends an average of $800 per prisoner, his expenses run $39,000 annually in medical care alone. Andrew Bowman, a 55-year-old serving time for bad checks, has only one kidney, severe diabetes, high blood pressure, gout, and circulatory problems. He requires 31 pills a day to stay alive and is expected to need dialysis in the near future.

These maintenance costs, however, are dwarfed by the expense of holding low-risk inmates in an overtaxed, overcrowded prison system. Without counting the needs of state correctional facilities, new cell space to handle the overflow in the Federal system alone will run between $3,800,000,000 and $5,500,000,000 for the estimated 57,000–83,000 new cells required by 1997. By the year 2000, a new cell will cost a projected

$200,000. At that price, those currently occupied by elderly prisoners will be as much as $4,000,000,000.

The most expensive cells are clearly those within maximum security facilities like Angola. Surrounded by 20-foot-high walls and topped with miles of concertina wire and numerous guard posts, these institutions are built for our most vicious criminals. It is ironic, therefore, to walk through these maximum security prisons and find geriatric inmates 70 and 80 years old—often confined to wheelchairs or hospital beds.

It is shocking to find men at Angola like Albert Crowe, who has spent more than two decades there for an offense he might not have committed in the first place. In the early 1960s, Crowe was a supervisor on an oil rig. He never had been arrested, had spent 14 years in the army, and was awarded both the Silver and Bronze Stars for bravery in Korea. One night in 1964, however, Crowe tried to blow his brains out. He had been experiencing emotional problems for some time and, when he recovered, Crowe went to the State Psychiatric Hospital and asked for help. He told the social worker that he needed psychiatric treatment, confessing that he had slept with his two daughters. The state arrested Crowe for incest and then offered him a "deal"—confess to aggravated rape and receive a life sentence. Crowe, who was told he could walk out of prison in seven years, pleaded guilty. He never had a trial. Now, he is 60 years old and requires constant medical attention for high blood pressure. As with Brown, his sentence is two to three times the average for murder.

Paroling Geriatric Prisoners

The Project for Older Prisoners (POPS) is the first organization in the country to work exclusively with the elderly and infirm. Composed of hundreds of law students in Washington, D.C., and Louisiana, it is examining the costs of this expanding geriatric prison population. The project is developing ways that states can lower expenses by acting to handle common geriatric problems. At the same time, POPS interviews and evaluates those who are low-risk candidates for release to help make cells available for more dangerous prisoners. Students compile pardon and parole cases that include guaranteed housing and benefits for the inmates upon their release. By identifying low-risk candidates for parole and confirming the necessary benefits needed to readjust to society, states (using this model) can open up thousands of cells while actually lowering the risk currently imposed on society by unguided court-ordered releases.

Early release clearly is out of the question for some. Mass murderers like John Wayne Gacy, Richard Speck, and Ted Bundy never will, or should, be released. Many of the elderly, however, fall into age and crime categories with very low likelihoods of committing new offenses. Nationwide, people between the age of 50 and 54 are responsible for 1.6 percent of new crimes; those 60 and over, .07 percent. Age is considered by the U.S. Parole Commission to be the one accurate predictor for recidivism (the tendency to commit a new offense). Within a year of their release, those between the ages of 18 and 24 have a recidivism rate of roughly 22 percent; for those over the age of 45, it is 2.1 percent.

Some of these prisoners have had no disciplinary write-ups in 10 or 15 years. Quenton Brown had only six in 18 years. The latest was for leaving a bottle of Maalox on his bunk. Another, a convicted murderer, only had two write-ups in 28 years. Both were for ministering to other prisoners without prior permission. Ironically, the nonviolent character of most elderly inmates makes them practically invisible in institutions that primarily are concerned with violent prisoners. Removing stable individuals from an otherwise volatile institution is hardly a priority.

Unfortunately for elderly inmates, they are not priorities for anyone. After Willie Horton, politicians view pardons and early releases with as much interest as drinking molten lead. While academics can show governors boxes of data demonstrating that elderly inmates are statistically safer than some parts of the population at large, prison policies are political first and only logical by accident. Governors prefer to let dangerous prisoners go rather than elderly ones for a simple reason—if a younger prisoner is released under a court order and kills someone, the courts (not the governors) are blamed.

This political theater can become almost vaudevillian at times. In New Orleans, a state agency has sued the local prison because it is overcrowded and in violation of state building codes. The facility is overcrowded because there are *state* inmates being held there since the state prison is overcrowded and under court order by a Federal agency. As a result, hundreds of young prisoners are released monthly. When President Bush called for a war on drugs, New Orleans responded by arresting dozens of dealers. Dozens of prisoners (including some drug dealers) were set free to accommodate the new arrivals. This charade is repeated in virtually every state in the country, since 42 and the District of Columbia are under court order to relieve prison overcrowding. Every day, young prisoners hit the streets, violent youths with a lot of time and inclination to commit another crime.

Seventy percent of these young prisoners will commit new offenses within three years of their early release. An example is Arthur Lewis, one of the 15,000 prisoners released early from New Orleans jails in a six-month period due to overcrowding. Only two months later, he allegedly gunned down a tourist in the French Quarter in front of the victim's wife and friends. The man apparently failed to hand over his wallet fast enough. At age 19, Lewis already had a record that included arrests for theft, burglary, and robbery, in addition to the auto theft charge that was pending at the time of the shooting.

Young releasees often are more dangerous than those who are serving long sentences for more serious crimes. Many of these long-term inmates are first-time offenders serving sentences that are two or three times the national average. Andrew Bowman was given 58 years for writing bad checks, even though complete restitution was made and he was a first-time offender. (The average sentence for murder for a first-time offender is less than nine years.) Bowman will cost the state tens of thousands of dollars a year in dialysis and other treatments. Although his wife, a nurse, could pay for all of her husband's treatment, Louisiana recently said no to releasing him.

Statistically, these long-term inmates are safer than younger prisoners who have committed a series of lesser offenses. Most young recidivists will continue a criminal pattern until age 30, when society will give them a long-term sentence. Ironically, it is at age 30 that most criminal patterns end. Consequently, the justice system waits until an individual is past his peak of criminal activity before he is given long-term incarceration. After considerable work, POPS secured releases for Brown, Hankins, and Crowe. One month after his parole, Willy Hankins died. Harvey Edwards died in prison. Bowman remains incarcerated.

State legislatures across the country continue to further the traditional policy towards overcrowding in correctional facilities—a mix of benign neglect and institutional ignorance. In the meantime, thousands of these forgotten inmates remain incarcerated, sad personifications of the outmoded, geriatric policies that keep them behind bars.

III. REINSTATING THE DEATH PENALTY

EDITOR'S INTRODUCTION

For a time the death penalty was discontinued in the U.S., but with the demand for tougher, harsher treatment of criminals it is again being used, and is as controversial as ever. In an article from *USA Today*, Cornelius F. Murphy provides the reader with the background of the Supreme Court's changing position regarding the death penalty. Conservatives like Supreme Court Justice Antonin Scalia have in recent decisions moved the Court toward the position of deferring to the states, thus allowing capital punishment to go forward. But, Murphy explains, the sentencing differences among the various states has created a bar to fair and equal treatment. He goes on to say that with fair and equal treatment not achievable, the Court has no choice but to rule against capital punishment altogether. Robert F. Drinan, in the next article, reprinted from *America*, defines the Catholic position on the death penalty. In 1980 Catholic bishops expressed their opposition to it, yet when polled, Catholics, like 70 percent of all Americans, generally supported it. Curiously, Catholics who are militantly pro-life, on grounds of the sanctity of life, also favor the imposition of the death penalty.

Writing in the *Humanist*, Barbara Dority reminds the reader that since 1976, when the Supreme Court lifted the ban on execution, 170 people have been put to death, and that another 2,600 are sitting on death rows in United States prisons. Dority goes on to condemn state killings, arguing that they are never a deterrent to crime and that they cost three times as much as a sentence of life imprisonment. Moreover, she points out, capital punishment discriminates against the poor and is racist. About 40 percent of death row inmates are black, whereas only 8 percent of the population as a whole is black. Richard Lacayo in an article from *Time* stresses that indigent defendants are at a considerable disadvantage in the legal system. Public defender offices may provide defense attorneys but they are often young, inexperienced, and without training in criminal law. By contrast, wealthy individuals are able to draw on the best legal minds available.

Finally, Susan Blaustein in a chilling article from *Harper's* describes her visit to Huntsville, Texas where prison executions by lethal injection are now being carried out routinely. A particularly gruesome feature of the trial system in Texas is that state law requires an inmate to produce new evidence of his innocence within thirty days of his conviction—an impossibly short time for a newly condemned person to procure trial transcripts (which might take longer than thirty days in itself), hire a new lawyer to reinvestigate the case, and file a motion for a new trial. Since 1976, not a single appeal for clemency on the grounds of innocence ever succeeded in Texas.

THE SUPREME COURT AND CAPITAL PUNISHMENT[1]

Much of the constitutional debate surrounding the death penalty concerns its compatibility with the Eighth Amendment's prohibition against the imposition of cruel and unusual punishment. Justice William Brennan, Jr., argued eloquently that the sentence of death offends both the dignity of the prisoner and the evolving standards of decency which reflect the advance of a maturing society. That position has not prevailed and, given the present composition of the Supreme Court, it is unlikely that it will in the foreseeable future.

Newer members, such as Justice Antonin Scalia, have a more restricted view of the Court's role in our society and fiercely resist any steps that would make the justices "philosopher-kings," rather than "judges of the law." The debate over whether the death penalty is inherently unjust, or offends civilized standards, undoubtedly will continue. Nevertheless, concentration upon the morality of capital punishment, however important in itself, can detract attention from less divisive issues of constitutional importance.

The justices of the Supreme Court are not Platonic guardians, but they all must recognize they have a responsibility to assure that no condemned prisoner be deprived of his life without due

[1] Article by Cornelius F. Murphy from *USA Today* Mr. '93. Copyright © 1993 by USA Today. Reprinted by permission.

process of law. The distinction is important because it will be
concerns over the administration of justice, rather than ideal
standards, which eventually may lead the Court to decide that the
death penalty is forbidden by the Constitution. To understand
why this is so requires a brief historical review.

In *Furman v. Georgia* (1972), the Supreme Court held that
capital punishment was being imposed "freakishly" and invali-
dated all state death penalty statutes then in force. In *Gregg v.
Georgia* (1976), it held that the death penalty was not unconstitutional in all circumstances. The judgment of the Court and the
opinion of Justice Potter Stewart acknowledged that the death
penalty can serve the social purposes of deterrence and retribution. The judgment also affirmed the Court's belief that sentencing discretion adequately could be guided to avoid the dangers of
arbitrary and capricious actions, which had led to the *Furman*
decision.

In the years immediately following *Gregg*, the Court strongly
asserted its authority as the nation's unique institution ultimately
responsible for the fair administration of capital justice. Between
1976 and 1982, it decided 15 capital cases on the merits. In all but
one, it reversed, and vacated, the death sentence as imposed. Its
decisions included a holding that punishment of death was a disproportionate penalty for rape (*Coker v. Georgia*), mandatory
death sentences for murder were unconstitutional (*Woodson v.
North Carolina*), and there must be a meaningful opportunity for
the sentencing authority to consider mitigating factors relative
either to the crime or the character of the individual offender
(*Lockett v. Ohio*). In this same period, the Court also decided that
vague instructions to a jury were constitutionally intolerable since
they did not provide sufficient assurance that a death sentence
would not be imposed wantonly (*Godfrey v. Georgia*) and invali-
dated restrictions on the defendant's access to information made
available to the sentencing power (*Gardner v. Florida*).

In May, 1979, the Supreme Court rejected a stay of execution
application of John Spenkelink. Some commentators insist that,
from that point on, the Court has been turning away from the
task of carefully reviewing the imposition of the death penalty. In
1983, this concern was expressed by Justice Thurgood Marshall.
Writing in dissent in *Zant v. Stephens,* he not only reiterated his
traditional position that the death penalty is unconstitutional in
all circumstances, he also chided the Court for not consistently
applying its earlier post-*Gregg* decisions.

While there is reason to believe the Court has lessened the rigors of its supervision over the imposition of the death penalty, it is difficult to determine exactly why this has happened. As the balance shifts to the conservative forces on the Court, the need to vindicate the criminal jurisdiction of the states has been emphasized. There is concern that executions are the only alternative to vigilante justice. As long as the imposition of capital punishment complied with the standards laid down in *Gregg* and subsequent decisions, the states were authorized constitutionally to carry out the death sentences. In the minds of some of the justices, persistent challenges to these sentences, particularly by collateral proceedings after direct review, were impairing both the rule of law and the integrity of state criminal trials. The reasoning seems to be that, when society determines certain murders are so terrible that those who perpetrate them deserve the penalty of death, such a determination should not be frustrated by the courts. While this point of view is understandable, it overlooks some of the more subtle aspects of constitutional responsibility that must be borne by a supreme judiciary.

No matter how legitimate the authority of states is to impose the death penalty, that power must be reconciled with the constitutional standards already laid down by the Supreme Court. Moreover, the legitimacy of the Court itself depends, in large measure, upon how faithfully the justices follow their own precedents. Once having said what the law is, the Court must be sure that it is upheld. This is particularly important in the capital punishment field, not only because of the nature of the penalty, but because its validation in *Gregg* was qualified by subsequent conditions laid down by the Court. In a number of recent cases, there has been a deep tension between the issues and the existing precedents. In resolving that tension, the Court too often has deferred to the power of the state to enact lethal retribution.

In *Clemons v. Mississippi*, for example, the State Supreme Court had upheld the death penalty even though one of the aggravating factors alleged by the state—that the crime was "especially heinous, atrocious, or cruel"—was unconstitutional under a prior decision of the U.S. Supreme Court. The latter, in an opinion by Justice Byron White, suggested that the State Appellate Tribunal could affirm the death penalty if it would find that a remaining valid aggravating factor outweighs the mitigating evidence. In *Blystone v. Pennsylvania*, the Court upheld a state statute which obligated the jury in a first degree murder case to impose the sentence of death if there was one aggravating circumstance and no mitigating circumstances; the aggravating circumstance was that the crime had been committed during the perpetration of a felony. In *Murray v. Giarratano,* it held that the principles of fundamental fairness secured by due process of law do not require a state to provide counsel to death row inmates who wish to pursue collateral post-conviction remedies.

In each of these cases, the Court majority has compromised the rule of law that had been established in earlier decisions. When sentencing by a state appellate court is approved, the principle of individualization of sentencing established in *Lockett* seriously is compromised. The individual has lost the full opportunity to be heard that is essential to due process of law. When the Court upheld the obligation to impose the death sentence in *Blystone,* it diluted its earlier decision in *Woodson v. North Carolina,* which held that mandatory death sentences are unconstitutional. In both instances, the legislature, rather than the jury, was given the ultimate authority to decide whether the death penalty, in a specific instance, was a deserved punishment. While the Court had been attentive to the accused's right to counsel at the trial stage of a capital case, its refusal to insist upon that right in collateral proceedings comprised the due process rights of the death row inmates.

In capital cases, direct review is not an adequate safeguard against miscarriages of justice. Collateral review of death sentences is indispensable, especially when assigned counsel at the earlier stages may not have prepared the case for the accused adequately. This need is borne out by statistics. In Federal noncapital *habeas corpus* petitions, relief is granted in less than 10 percent of the cases; in capital petitions, the success rate is more than 50 percent. To leave an ordinary person to his own resources in filing such petitions, as the Court did in *Murray,* is to deny such an individual the assistance that traditionally has been considered part of due process of law. The absence of counsel from the beginning of collateral proceedings will make it unlikely that all meritorious claims will be considered.

"Deregulating" the death penalty?

In fairness to the Supreme Court, it must not be implied that a majority of its members deliberately have "deregulated" the death penalty. For example, it has struck down state laws which would require unanimity before mitigating circumstances could be considered (*McKoy v. North Carolina*) and generally has tried to see that the penalty imposed in capital cases constituted a reasoned moral response to the character and personal history of the accused, as well as the crime itself. The Court has used that principle to strike down a politically popular law that would have mandated execution when a person serving a life sentence without possibility of parole is convicted of murder (*Summer v. Shuman*).

It may be more accurate to say that the Court increasingly is finding it difficult, if not impossible, to strike a balance between the need for a prompt enforcement of the death penalty and the necessity of careful and judicious review of the sentence. As new issues keep arising each term, the number of variables of fact and law the justices must take into account to fulfill its responsibilities place a serious strain on their capacities for impartial judgment. They are haunted by *Furman*, with its condemnation of unbridled discretion, yet seem unable to assure that those authorized to impose the death sentence exercise an authentic choice. In deferring to the states, they have weakened their independent authority. By allowing states to execute persons for crimes committed when they were 16 (*Stanford v. Kentucky*), or those mentally retarded (*Penny v. Lynaugh*), the Court has begun to lose sight of that ultimate responsibility for justice in capital cases that it assumed in *Gregg v. Georgia*. It even has ruled that evidence of disparate racial impact is insufficient grounds to reverse a death sentence (*McCleskey v. Kemp*).

Pending legislation would restrict the amount of post-conviction relief available to a condemned prisoner, but this only would exacerbate the problem. One may grant the need for a greater measure of finality, but what is of central importance is the need to make sure that, before any sentence is carried out, there will be a fair and complete judicial review. Given the qualitative difference between death and other punishments, there must be a measure of review commensurate with the gravity of the penalty. The Court, in conscience, can not allow the penalty of death unless the rights of the individual prisoner are respected fully.

While developing decisions concerning the death penalty are moving the constitutional compass back towards *Furman*, they also are weakening some of the premises of *Gregg*. The number of murders committed in the U.S. after the latter case remains about the same as it was before—approximately 20,000 per year.

Therefore, there is no proof that the death penalty provides an effective deterrent. In addition, the retributive value of capital punishment diminishes with the passage of time. While there are over two thousand inmates on death row, less than 10 percent have been executed since 1976. It is virtually impossible to distinguish, in a meaningful way, between those who will die and those who will remain in prison. Thus, there is a serious question whether the retention of the death penalty continues to serve any legitimate public purpose.

Retired Justice Lewis Powell has suggested that the time may have arrived when the Congress and state legislatures should consider ending such a "haphazard" practice as capital punishment. However, that responsibility falls upon the Supreme Court, for, while validating public execution, it also has insisted that capital punishment must be imposed "fairly, and with reasonable consistency, *or not at all*" (*Eddington v. Oklahoma*).

The uniqueness of the Court's role is its responsibility to make sure that the life of the individual is not taken without due process of law. The justices may differ over the meaning of human dignity and may be skeptical of their power to discern U.S. society's evolving standards of civilized behavior, but they share a common responsibility for the administration of justice. The death penalty may, or may not, be inherently unjust, but it should be declared unconstitutional because the Supreme Court is unable to supervise the imposition of the penalty properly. It no longer can fulfill that obligation of stringent review the Court imposed upon itself as the price of allowing the practice to continue.

CATHOLICS AND THE DEATH PENALTY[2]

Every public opinion poll in the United States on the death penalty shows that Catholics do not differ from non-Catholics in their view of the morality of the death penalty. Some 70 percent of all Americans favor it.

Yet the official Catholic position on capital punishment has

    [2] Article by Robert F. Drinan from *America* Je. 18, '94. Copyright © 1994 by America. Reprinted by permission.

become one of clear opposition. The Catholic bishops condemned the death penalty in 1980. The new *Catechism of the Catholic Church* states that, since the taking of a life must be the last and only available way to carry out a legitimate need of the state, the death penalty can rarely if ever be morally justified.

The conservative Catholic theologian Germain Grisez summed up the evolution of Catholic thought on the death penalty in this statement, written in 1993:

In the past, capital punishment sometimes may have seemed justified as a defensive measure. . . . Today, however, this defensive function plainly can be served in other ways. Thus, it is hardly possible to see how the use of the death penalty can be reconciled with Christian conceptions of human dignity and the sanctity of every human life. . . . It seems that Catholic teaching on capital punishment can develop, as [did the teaching] on coercion in matters of religion and on slavery (*The Way of the Lord Jesus: Vol. II. Living a Christian Life.* Franciscan Press, 1993).

Catholic bishops in the United States have in the recent past repeatedly and forcefully echoed that sentiment. On February 15 of this year [1994], the bishops of New York, in a statement released by Cardinal John O'Connor, president of the state's Catholic Conference, termed the death penalty "an affront to the human dignity of both those on whom it is inflicted and those in whose name it is employed."

The bishops of Indiana likewise stressed the multiple effects of the death penalty in their January 1994 statement that "lethal punishment, instead of protecting society, may even accelerate the cycle of violence." The bishops added that the death penalty "teaches society that violence is the answer to difficult human problems."

In the same month, the bishops of Kansas spoke out against capital punishment in the midst of a current legislative battle in which proponents of the death penalty are seeking to reinstate it in Kansas for the first time since 1972. The Kansas bishops stated that the death penalty "fuels vengeance, diverts from forgiveness, and greatly diminishes respect for all human life."

A book entitled *The Death Penalty Repudiated: A Tale of Two Catechisms* by James J. Megivern of the University of North Carolina meticulously traces the church's support for the death penalty from the time of Emperor Constantine I in the fourth century up until the 1930s. A reexamination of the church's position was stimulated by encyclicals of Pope Pius XII and Pope John XXIII and by documents issued at the Second Vatican Council.

Catholic officials in Europe and Latin America did not oppose, and sometimes approved, the abolition of the death penalty by the nations of these continents over the last generation.

Opposition to the death penalty by Catholic authorities in the United States began in 1971 when the National Catholic Conference for Interracial Justice and the National Coalition of American Nuns joined 11 other religious bodies in filing a brief in the U.S. Supreme Court urging that the death penalty be ruled unconstitutional. In 1974, the U.S. Catholic Conference deliberated about the death penalty for three days and, despite differences of approach, adopted a resolution that it go on record as opposed to capital punishment.

In 1977, Cincinnati's Archbishop Joseph Bernardin, then the president of the U.S.C.C. and later Cardinal Archbishop of Chicago, warned that a return to capital punishment "can only lead to further erosion of respect for life and to the increased brutalization of society." In 1980 the U.S. Catholic bishops, by a vote of 145 to 31 with 41 abstentions, urged that the death penalty be abolished.

It is sad to have to conclude that neither the nation's Catholics nor the public at large are heeding the church's condemnation of the death penalty. The number of executions continues to rise. In fact, there are now 2,760 men and forty-two women on death row. Thirty-two of the men were under the age of 18 at the time the offense occurred.

From 1976 to 1993, 225 men and one woman were put to death. Southern states led the way in the number of executions: 31.4 percent of the total occurred in Texas, 14.2 percent in Florida and 9.3 percent in Louisiana. Thirty-six of the 50 states have death penalty laws, although 15 of those states carried out no executions during this period.

Of the 226 executed, 88 were black and 14 were Latino. Nine were under the age of 18 at the time the offense occurred. In the same period (1976–93), 45 persons on death row were freed after they produced new evidence demonstrating that they were not guilty.

The pattern of racial discrimination in the carrying out of the death penalty has become notorious. Amnesty International, which continues to wage a worldwide struggle against the death penalty, notes that 40 percent of death row prisoners are black, although only 12 percent of the United States population is African-American. In addition, an amazing 84 percent of all persons executed since 1977 were charged with killing white victims, although black and white people are murdered in about equal numbers.

There is also a strong anti-male component in the way in which the death penalty is administered. Forty percent of the homicides in the country were committed by women, but only 1 percent of those on death row are female. Since 1930 there have been 3,873 persons executed, but only 32 of these were women.

The anxiety about crime in the United States is so strong at present that it is not clear that the majority in Congress or the country can even hear the solidly logical and legal arguments against capital punishment. The crime bill that has already passed the Senate and will be agreed to in some form by the House and the President contains some 50 new grounds for inflicting the death penalty. The new F.B.I. director, a Catholic, Louis Freeh, stated in February of this year [1994] that the death penalty is not a deterrent to crime. But even that testimony has not impeded the rush to have more executions and to have them more expeditiously.

For some time, America's Catholic bishops have advanced the "seamless garment" argument—the idea that life is so precious and inviolable that abortion, capital punishment, and destruction by nuclear weapons cannot be tolerated by the state. All the same, Catholics who are militantly pro-life, like Representative Henry Hyde (R., Ill.), favor the death penalty. Moreover, the virtual disappearance of the possibility of using nuclear weapons weakens the attraction of the "seamless garment" approach.

Is there any argument that could be effectively employed by Catholic leaders to alter the minds of the 70 percent of America's 59 million Catholics who favor the death penalty? One argument that could be appealing would compare the United States to other nations that still execute criminals. China is the leader in that category, with about four executions a day. This penalty is not, however, deterring rampant crime in China. Another argument is based on the deepening sense among jurists that capital punishment is now arguably a violation of customary international law and the practice of the majority of advanced nations.

Opposition to the death penalty is not a part of the official theological doctrine of the church. But it is more and more a part of the absolute reverence for life that is taught universally by the church. It is therefore disappointing and disconcerting that, in the United States, Catholic public opinion on capital punishment does not seem to be influenced by the church's position on this question.

The Catholic bishops of New York said it well in their statement of Feb. 15, 1994: "Capital punishment is the easy way out of addressing the complex, pervasive, and expensive problems which surround us. The death penalty is no more the answer for violent crime than abortion is the answer to unplanned pregnancies. Death is never the answer."

NOT IN MY NAME[3]

It is 12:30 A.M. on Tuesday morning, January 5, 1993. Just minutes ago, in the gallows room at the Walla Walla state penitentiary, officials of Washington state placed a black hood over the head and shoulders of convicted child rapist and murderer Westley Allan Dodd. They bound his hands and feet with straps, carefully knotted a rope under his jaw, sprang the trap door on which he stood, and hanged him by his neck until he was dead. According to most witnesses (after over one hundred reporters vied for the privilege, the lucky ones were chosen by lottery), the procedure was "surreal, sterile, efficient, and amazingly swift."

For many weeks, the media has been in a macabre frenzy in anticipation of the obscene and sickening spectacle: the first execution by hanging in the United States since 1965. This ritual murder was performed on behalf of Washington's citizens and in our names, using our tax monies, our employees, even our rope. In return, we were able to witness our state committing a detached, brutal, premeditated homicide.

This barbarity was cheered on by a sizable crowd outside the penitentiary. Many wore nooses around their necks, and some carried signs: "Hang Him High!" "Kill Him!" and "Let Dodd Dangle!" They wrote "HANG HIM!" in huge letters in the snow and sang, "All we are saying, is give death a chance." At 12:01 A.M., the scheduled time of death, they cheered, set off firecrackers, and opened bottles of champagne.

This was the first execution in Washington state since 1963.

---

[3] Article by Barbara Dority from *The Humanist* Mr./Ap. '93. Copyright © 1993 by The Humanist. Reprinted by permission.

Dodd was the first of 12 prisoners the state is moving to execute. Because his crimes were so heinous, and because he repeatedly said that he wanted to be hanged and rebuffed any efforts to prevent it, many feel that we who oppose the death penalty were wrong in trying to prevent the state from killing him.

Last night, numerous experts were paraded before the television cameras; all of them said that Dodd was a sadistic psychopathic pedophile incapable of empathy, that his greatest fear was being "a nobody," and that he had successfully manipulated us into making him "a somebody" via the sensational media coverage of his hanging.

Did it therefore make moral sense to do what this deranged human being wanted us to do? Should we have abetted him in his final vile crime—that of making murderers out of us as well? Henry Schwarzchild of the National Coalition to Abolish the Death Penalty points out that execution—even when "consensual"—is not a state-assisted suicide but, rather, prisoner-assisted homicide. (If prisoners attempt to actually commit *suicide*, the state intervenes to prevent it.)

Abolitionists maintain that the state has no right to kill anyone; a prisoner's death wish cannot grant a right not otherwise possessed. The right to reject life imprisonment and choose death should be respected, but it changes nothing for those of us who oppose that death *at the hands of the state*.

Over 2,600 people are sitting on death rows in the United States—more than at any time in our history. Since 1930, when the federal government began collecting such data, over 3,900 executions have been recorded. Since 1976, when the Supreme Court lifted the ban on execution, 170 people have been killed. Because these official killings have been perpetrated in our names, it is every American's responsibility to give careful consideration to the facts regarding this crucial issue.

The death penalty is irrational—a fact that should carry considerable weight with rationalists. And, as Albert Camus pointed out, "Capital punishment . . . has always been a religious punishment and is irreconcilable with humanism." In other words, this archaic and barbarous "custom" comes to us from the cruel "eye for an eye" anti-human caves of religion—another factor that should raise immediate misgivings for freethinkers.

State killings are morally bankrupt. Why do we kill people to show other people that killing people is wrong? We become complicit with murderers when we replicate their deeds. Would we

allow rape as the penalty for rape—or the burning of arsonists'
homes as the penalty for arson?

The state should never have the power to murder its subjects. To give
the state this power eliminates the individual's most effective
shield against the tyranny of the majority and is inconsistent with
democratic principles.

*Families and friends of murder victims are further victimized by state
killings.* Quite a few leaders in the movement to abolish the death
penalty became involved specifically *because* someone they loved
was murdered. One of these, Marie Deans, says:

> The violence of murder is abhorrent, but the long sequence of trials and
> appeals that ultimately lead to another killing is not a solution but a
> process of carrying on violence. While it goes on, the family lives a day-to-
> day existence focused on the death of their loved one. Somehow we must
> find a better, more humane way to deal with murder, a way that does not
> twist sorrow into vengeance and memory into nightmare.

The families of Dodds' three victims—as well as members of
his own family—repeatedly stated they wanted him to die. One of
their main reasons—in addition to the desire for justice (read:
vengeance)—was that they wanted it to be over; they didn't ever
want to see Dodd's picture or hear or read his words in the media
again. Yet, if it weren't for the sensationalism attending the death
penalty itself, the media exposure (and, in most cases, the many
years of appeals) would not occur in the first place.

Instead, people like Dodd would be quietly and safely put
away for life with *absolutely no* possibility for parole (a perfectly
attainable goal already being implemented in many states where
the death penalty has been abolished).

*The death penalty violates constitutional prohibitions against cruel
and unusual punishment.* The grotesque gassing of Robert Harris
by the state of California on April 21, 1992, and similar reports of
witnesses to hangings and lethal injections should leave no doubt
that the dying process can be—and often is—grossly inhumane,
regardless of the method.

The death penalty is applied arbitrarily—and often for political gain.
For instance, during his presidential campaign, Bill Clinton
rushed home for the Arkansas execution of Rickey Ray Rector, a
mentally retarded, indigent black man. Clinton couldn't take the
chance of being seen by the voters as "soft on crime." And of the
approximately 20,000 people arrested for murder each year in
the United States, hundreds whose crimes are just as repugnant
as those on death rows are spared and receive lighter sentences.

Capital punishment discriminates against the poor. Although murderers come from all classes, those on death row are almost without exception poor and were living in poverty at the time they were arrested. The majority of death-row inmates were or are represented by court-appointed public defenders—and the state is not obligated to provide an attorney at all for appeals beyond the state level.

The application of capital punishment is racist. About 40 percent of death-row inmates are black, whereas only 8 percent of the population as a whole are black. In cases with white victims, black defendants were four to six times more likely to receive death sentences than white defendants who had similar criminal histories. Studies show that the chance for a death sentence is five to 10 times greater in cases with white victims than with black victims. In the criminal-justice system, the life of a white person is worth more than the life of a black person.

The mentally retarded are victimized by the death penalty. Since 1989, when the Supreme Court upheld state killing of the mentally retarded, at least four such executions have occurred. According to the Southern Center for Human Rights, at least 10 percent of death-row inmates in the United States are mentally retarded.

Juveniles are subject to the death penalty. Since state execution of juveniles also became permissible in the decision cited above, at least five people who were juveniles when their crimes were committed have been executed.

Innocent people can be—and have been—executed. With the death penalty, errors are irreversible. According to a 1987 study, 23 people who were innocent of the crimes for which they were convicted were executed between 1900 and 1985. Until human judgment becomes infallible, this problem alone is reason enough to abolish the death penalty at the hands of a state more dedicated to vengeance than to truth and justice.

The death penalty is not an effective deterrent and, in fact, creates an atmosphere that encourages and fosters violence. Studies comparing homicide rates in death-penalty states with those in other states show that the death penalty does not lower the murder rate. And the number of police, prison guards, and inmates killed is higher in death-penalty states. We continue to have shockingly higher rates of murder than do western European nations, none of which practice capital punishment.

The vast majority of murders are irrational, passionate acts perpetrated by uncontrolled rage and/or while under the influence of alcohol or drugs. The possible threat of death in the distant future has no effect on a person in that irrational state.

Executions do not save money. There are those who cry that we, the taxpayers, shouldn't have to "support" condemned people for an entire lifetime in prison—that we should simply "eliminate" them and save ourselves the time and money. The truth is that the cost of state killing is up to three times the cost of lifetime imprisonment. Judges and others are reluctant—as they should be—to shorten the execution process for fear that hasty procedures will lead to the execution of more innocent persons.

Studies show a general correlation between a nation's utilization of capital punishment and a general disregard for human rights. The United States is the only western nation to practice capital punishment on a large scale, thus putting us in the company of Iran and South Africa, as well as placing us on Amnesty International's list of nations with governmental policies violating human rights.

We cannot rely upon the courts stacked as they now are with death penalty advocates. We must refuse to be made into passive co-conspirators in state homicide. It's up to each of us to tell our government in no uncertain terms: *"Do not kill in my name."*

YOU DON'T ALWAYS GET PERRY MASON[4]

With two powerful jolts of electricity, Roger Keith Coleman was executed [in December 1991] in Virginia. But the questions about his guilt could not so easily be disposed of—in part because his court-appointed lawyers failed to put them to rest at his trial. On the night that Wanda Fay McCoy was murdered, Coleman claimed to have been at several points around the coal-mining town of Grundy. Shouldn't his lawyers have tried to retrace his steps on that night and search out witnesses? Shouldn't they have ventured into McCoy's or Coleman's home? At the very least, shouldn't they have presented to the jury the bag of bloody sheets and two cowboy shirts McCoy's neighbor found a few days after the murder?

[4] Article by Richard Lacayo from *Time* Je. 1, '92. Copyright © 1992 by Time Inc. Reprinted by permission.

Over six years ago, Jesus Romero was sentenced to death for taking part in the 1984 gang rape and murder of a 15-year-old in San Benito, Texas. He might have been sent to a mental hospital instead if his court-appointed attorney had presented available evidence to the jury that supported an insanity defense. "His lawyer had no idea there was information available that Romero was completely insane at the time of the crime," contends Nick Trenticosta, who handled Romero's appeals. During the course of his appeals, a lower federal court ruled that Romero had received ineffective counsel at his trial, but a higher appeals court reversed that ruling. Last week Romero died by injection in Huntsville, Texas.

Accused killers don't tend to be attractive people. Quite a few of them, perhaps the overwhelming majority, are guilty. But even the most dubious characters are supposed to get a fair trial, in which their attorneys are equipped to make the best possible case on their behalf. Because the majority of murder defendants are also broke, however, many of them get court-appointed lawyers who lack the resources, experience, or inclination to do their utmost. When the Supreme Court restored capital punishment in 1976, it did so in the expectation that death sentences would be imposed in a fair and equitable manner. It hasn't always worked that way. Some people go to traffic court with better prepared lawyers than many murder defendants get. And yet no case carries higher stakes than a murder trial in the 36 states where the death penalty is legal.

The question of who defends accused killers has become more urgent lately. In a series of recent cases, the Supreme Court has been closing off the paths through which death-row inmates get federal appeals courts to review—and review again—their convictions. That creates more pressure to ensure fair trials in the first place. Perhaps the most serious restriction yet may be handed down in a Virginia case, *Wright v. West*. That case could permit the justices to rule, in effect, that federal appeals judges should work mostly from the assumption that the courtroom rulings of state-level trial judges are correct. The result would be to limit sharply the kind of questions the federal courts can reopen on appeal.

"What the Supreme Court is saying now is states have got remarkably better at guaranteeing certain liberties," says Ira Robbins, a habeas corpus specialist at Washington's American University law school. In the state courthouses, where the trials are held, however, the guarantee of competent counsel looks rather threadbare. Some cities maintain public-defender offices to provide attorneys to indigent defendants. Well-funded offices can often afford attorneys who specialize in criminal law and even capital crimes. But a number of states—including several Southern states with the nation's highest execution rates—use a shakier system of court-appointed lawyers selected from a list of local attorneys. Many are either young attorneys fresh out of school or older ones who ordinarily specialize in the bread-and-butter work of title searches or divorce litigation.

Though appeals courts have been lenient in ruling that defense attorneys have done an adequate job—judges deemed meritless all of Coleman's claims of ineffective assistance by counsel—it's the rare court-appointed lawyer who is skilled in the complexities of capital cases. "This is a highly specialized area of law," says Harold G. Clarke, chief justice of the Georgia Supreme Court, who has reviewed many death sentences. "Even a good criminal lawyer may not have had much, if any, experience in capital cases." Court-appointed attorneys must also be willing to settle for modest fees that rarely cover the cost of a thorough defense. While a private attorney in Atlanta may make upwards of $75 an hour, court-appointed lawyers in Georgia are paid about $30 an hour. In Alabama they cannot be paid more than $1,000 for pretrial preparations. Even if they spend just 500 hours at the task—the U.S. average in 1987 was 2,000—that amounts to $2 an hour. "The lawyer would be better off going to work at McDonald's," says Stephen Bright, director of the Southern Center for Human Rights.

Many of them are also unhappy to find themselves defending accused killers whose victims may be familiar to their neighbors. Nor does it help to know that, if convicted, their clients will have an incentive to turn against them later. Claims of ineffective counsel are a staple of appeals filings—not only because mediocre lawyering is so common but also because the accusation is a reliable way to gain the attention of appeals courts. That's one reason prosecutors and some defense attorneys scoff at claims that capital-case lawyering is all that bad. "The competency-of-counsel issue has been totally blown out of proportion," says Marvin White Jr., a Mississippi assistant attorney general. "Counsel in the majority of cases has been competent and effective."

That claim is sharply contested by defendants'-rights advocates. "It's not just once in a while that you see a lawyer make a mistake," insists Charles Hoffman, an Illinois public defender who pursues appeals for death-row inmates. "It's over and over and over again." It's easy for inexperienced lawyers to make a mistake. Under the rules established by a 1977 Supreme Court decision, lawyers in a criminal case must recognize potential violations of fair procedure as soon as they take place and raise the objection in court. If they fail to do so during the trial, they may forfeit the chance for their client to raise the issue on appeal. "People talk about criminals often getting off on technicalities," says Hoffman. "Actually, a lot of people are dying because of technicalities."

Some of the worst errors are made during what is called the penalty phase. This is a separate hearing, following a guilty verdict, in which the jury in a capital case must choose between a prison sentence and the death penalty. Prosecutors offer evidence of "aggravating factors" such as excessive cruelty to convince the jury that the convicted killer should be executed. Defense lawyers are supposed to point out "mitigating factors"—evidence of mental disability, for example, or a history of childhood abuse—that might lead a jury to choose life in prison. But tracking down the evidence of a client's past is time-consuming and expensive, often requiring the services of social workers, psychologists and investigators whom poorly funded defenders cannot afford to hire.

Seeking to remedy this problem, the Federal Government recently established 15 death-penalty resource centers around the country. Supported by $11.5 million a year in federal funds, as well as state matching funds, the centers recruit, train and assist lawyers who handle appeals for convicts on death row. But attorneys from those centers enter only after conviction, not at the trial, where the Supreme Court now requires that most crucial issues be recognized and raised.

Proposals for similar centers to improve lawyering at the trial phase have gone nowhere. Nor do death-penalty opponents see much hope in the idea of "mandatory pro bono," a system that would require all lawyers and firms to donate some time to representing poor defendants. An attorney who ordinarily specializes in corporate cases or real estate, no matter how competent or well trained, would still be at sea amid the complexities of a murder trial. Says Shelly O'Neill, a Reno public defender: "It's like calling a dentist to do a brain surgeon's work."

Some experts say a better reform would be for more states to establish public-defender offices, in rural as well as urban areas, and provide them with sufficient funds. Though the $2.2 million annual budget of the Reno office, financed by Washoe County, is far from lavish, it is still enough to afford a permanent staff of 19 attorneys, six of whom are qualified by training and substantial trial experience to handle capital cases.

The Reno operation also has access to some of the same resources that local district attorneys rely on. "If we need an expert from Washington to come testify," O'Neill explains, "we can get the funds from the county to bring him or her in." With those advantages, the Reno office has saved three capital defendants from lethal injection in the past two years.

Reno's approach could be duplicated elsewhere. But are budget-strapped states really likely to pour money into better court defense for accused killers? It's hardly a vote getter. And it's not cheap. But neither is capital punishment. If the U.S. wants the death penalty, it will have to pay what it costs to guarantee each defendant the highest level of fairness and equality—or sacrifice its own standards of justice.

WITNESS TO ANOTHER EXECUTION[5]

The road from Austin to Huntsville, Texas, runs past oil rigs and tin-roofed homes whose ramshackle porches sag under the weight of old refrigerators and trailer parts, past red barns and white fences and hand-painted signs advertising Brahman Bulls and Suzie's Bar-B-Q, and on a quiet evening last August, following the road by a succession of tiny Baptist graveyards and watching the swifts dive and glide in the deepening blue, I noticed an anti-littering sign (DON'T MESS WITH TEXAS!) and remembered why I was driving northeast. After that night, at least one man wouldn't be messing with Texas any time soon, and I was going to witness his execution.

Outwardly a sleepy little southern town, Huntsville is surrounded by seven prisons that house 11,800 inmates, 376 of them locked in five-by-nine-foot cells awaiting their carefully premeditated, supposedly painless, government-administered deaths.

[5] Article by Susan Blaustein from *Harper's Magazine* My. '94. Copyright © 1994 by Harper's Magazine. Reprinted by permission.

The Texas Department of Criminal Justice, known as the TDC, is Huntsville's principal industry, and during the busier seasons the state executes as many as two men a week, making the town the nation's capital of capital punishment. As a member of the press pool, I planned to attend the execution later that night of Carl Eugene "Bo" Kelly of Waco, Texas, who had spent twelve years under sentence of death for his part in the brutal murder of two young men. The series of efforts by Kelly's lawyers to get his execution stayed—on the grounds that he had suffered brain damage as a result of severe childhood abuse; that he had been high on barbiturates, Valium, marijuana, and alcohol at the time of his crime; that he was improperly compelled by police to confess and sentenced more harshly than his accomplice; that he had been heartwarmingly rehabilitated—had all failed. That morning, in Austin, the governor's office had informed Kelly's lead attorney, Rob Owen, that his client's chances of executive clemency were slim.

The town square was deserted, but beyond its one-block stretch of quaintly renovated shops I found a glowing white Dairy Queen in which two female prison guards, both of them in gray uniforms, were sharing gossip and ice-cream sundaes. The DQ is just a block from the Walls Unit, which houses the death chamber where, by state law, all executions in Texas must be carried out, but neither guard knew that another convict was scheduled to die later that night, "at any time," in the language of the statute, "before the hour of sunrise." Nor did the crowd at Zach's, a college hangout ten blocks away, where students from Sam Houston State University (known locally as Sam) were eating nachos and shooting pool. The university (the second largest business in town) is known nationally for its fine criminal justice center, which graduates hundreds of "CJ" majors and where active-duty TDC officials are trained. Like the prison guards, the students at Zach's didn't much care that a man was going to be executed in Huntsville that night, but a freshman dance major volunteered that an escaped convict had taken a female student hostage a few weeks back. One bright-eyed CJ major named Kevin Pooler said that because two of his buddies had been murdered recently in Houston he had no qualms about capital punishment.

"Burn 'em, fry 'em!" shrugged Pooler, who said he hoped to become a prosecutor and then a Supreme Court justice. "So what if a few innocent people slip through. That's better than having a lot of guilty people on the street! If criminals start seeing people getting popped off after six months, I'm sorry, but that's going to change some minds."

The state of Texas apparently has taken its cue from citizens like Pooler. A poll conducted in 1992 by a group of Texas newspapers found that 79 percent of the state's citizens favor the death penalty. Since 1976, when the Supreme Court ruled the death penalty constitutional (thereby resurrecting execution in the United States after a four-year hiatus), seventy-two men have been executed in Huntsville—more than twice as many as in Florida, the next most productive state in the execution market, and more than three times as many as in Virginia and Louisiana, which rank third and fourth. In the last two years, the rate of Texas executions has more than tripled, and the seventeen men executed in 1993 alone constitute nearly a fourth of those put to death since executions resumed in Texas in 1982.

At 8:00 P.M. I called Kelly's lawyers, who told me that his petition had been denied by the U.S. Court of Appeals for the Fifth Circuit and that a new appeal had just been faxed to the Supreme Court. This, I knew, meant that Kelly's chances for a stay of execution had all but vanished, but, as it so happened, I didn't see him die. The wire services and the Texas press had filled the five available places in the media pool—that pale reminder of the once madding crowd that for centuries has reveled in witnessing the grim administration of justice. Prison officials assured me, however, that I wouldn't have to wait long for my turn, what with twenty-four more executions scheduled in the next eight weeks. When the death penalty was reactivated here, the first executions were mobbed. Now they have become so commonplace that few turn out for them. Nonetheless, I decided to post myself outside the Walls Unit, which was cordoned off to keep out possible rabble-rousers, to see who might show up to mark Carl Kelly's death.

Built in 1849 and by the turn of the century decked out with tropical atrium gardens, turrets, porticoes, and a clock tower that the whole town told time by, Texas's aptly named oldest prison is now a faceless brick bunker flanked by forty-foot walls topped by razor wire. A lone guard manned the corner tower, beneath which a dozen anti-death-penalty demonstrators, known locally as Amnesty people because of the affiliation some of them have with Amnesty International, had gathered for their sober candlelight vigil. By 11:20 prison officials learned that the Supreme Court had unanimously denied Kelly a stay. Shortly before midnight the official witnesses filed inside the Walls to the polite din of the protesters' pots, pans, and wooden flutes. Suddenly, two pickups roared into the parking lot, spewing out drunken college students who launched into raucous, inebriated choruses of "You're on the highway to hell" and "So long, farewell, auf wiedersehen, fuck you."

"Get a life!" a young woman hollered at the Amnesty people as she drove by. "We're trying to save one!" one demonstrator responded meekly. When one of the students asked who was being killed and why, and how the protesters would feel had the inmate's victim been their mother, he was quickly regaled with anti-death-penalty statistics; Carl Kelly's case never came up.

At 12:27 A.M. the witnesses emerged from the Walls, reporting that Kelly had been pronounced dead at 12:22; that he had requested wild game for his last meal but instead was given hamburgers, water, and fries (which he didn't eat); and that his last words were, "I'm an African warrior, born to bleed, born to die." (The mother of one of Kelly's victims was not impressed when I read his final words to her over the phone. "Oh yeah, right," she said. "What about the rest of us? When I heard he said that, any feelings I might have had for him just kinda snapped and I said, 'Okay, justice has been served.'")

Ask anyone in Huntsville and he or she will tell you that the rapid clip of executions has absolutely nothing to do with life there. "It's just not our issue," explained City Manager Gene Pipes. "This is the state carrying out a legal mandate that has nothing to do with the local community. It happens to be DATELINE, HUNTSVILLE, but it's just not what's being talked about on the square."

Indeed, the morning after Kelly's execution there was no sign anywhere near the square that anything unusual had happened. The yellow tape outside the Walls was gone; across the street, in their telltale white prison suits, trusties were mowing the lawn and hosing down the family car at the TDC director's vast, neo-Georgian mansion. At the Cafe Texan, the regular 9:30 coffee crowd of retired white ranchers and constables joshed with a sassy veteran waitress and rehashed old cowboy yarns, while black workers shouldered trays of steaming, clean dishware and ate in the kitchen. At the Masonic Lodge coffee klatch, a group of mostly older men (a TDC guard, a cook, a retired chaplain, an engineer, the county judge, the founder of the local John Birch Society, and a retired crime-scene photographer) took it upon

themselves to explain that Huntsville had been called the Rome of
Texas, built as it was on seven hills and seven creeks, as well as the
Athens of Texas, because the state's first law school and teachers
college were founded here. Huntsville's founders donated the
land for the state penitentiary, confident that legislators would
then also locate the state capital there, but the Texas legislature,
by one vote, chose Austin, and the disappointed Huntsville citi-
zenry had to content itself with the eleven horse thieves who were
the Walls' first reluctant guests.

Over the course of the next few weeks, while waiting my turn
to witness an execution, I discovered that most of the people in
town preferred to know as little as possible about Huntsville's
main industry. "This is a marvelous place to raise a family," said
Jane Monday, a former mayor and historian. "It's a university
town, a town that cares a great deal about its young; it's warm, it's
cozy, it's a very caring community. I wouldn't take a million dollars
to live anywhere else." When I asked about the effect all of Huntsville's prisons and executions had on its young, Monday shook
her head firmly. "It might sound funny to you, but I don't think it
affects the children or the community at all."

City Councilman Jimmy Carter at first agreed. "That's the
prison system," he said automatically when I asked why no one in
Huntsville seemed to bother about executions. "The town is very
distinct from that. Or maybe that's just part of our defense mech-
anism. We don't want to identify with executions or acknowledge
that we are involved with that in any way."

Tommy Cole, a physician whose great-grandfather headed
the TDC and whose family home has abutted the Walls for more
than a century, admitted that he too is unaware of the executions.
Dr. Cole likened himself to those living in small towns outside
Nazi death camps. "We just visited Weimar, a few miles outside of
Buchenwald, and no one there had any idea what went on, just
like we have no idea what goes on behind those walls over there,"
he volunteered over a scotch in his fuchsia-damasked living room,
in which much of the elegantly carved antique furniture was
made by prison labor.

The obliviousness of townspeople to the executions was notable, but more striking was the way in which career TDC employees involved in the work managed to keep it from impinging on
their consciousness. "It's real simple: I either do my job or I don't
eat," the assistant director for public information, Charles L.
Brown, told me when I asked how he felt about witnessing every

execution. "My position is purely defensible: if I'm going to have to answer questions about it, I ought to be there. It's got nothing to do with my feelings about the death penalty; I'm just doing my job professionally and to the best of my ability. It works perfect, in that regard. And nobody would know whether I'm for or against capital punishment. You'd be surprised," Brown added, "how many people here are opposed to capital punishment."

I asked the same question of Brother Cecil McKee, a retired Walls Unit chaplain whose job it was to walk condemned men to the electric chair until the U.S. Supreme Court effectively placed a moratorium on executions in 1972. "It was hard to be there, but I didn't have to see it," he told me. "I closed my eyes . . . You know, the flesh burns—it leaves a terrible odor. I'd go home and take my clothes off, leave 'em out, we'd go to sleep. Next day, I had to send my clothes to the cleaners. It was just part of the job."

I asked Brother McKee how he felt about assisting the state in taking lives. He looked at me with watery blue eyes. "I've never said this before: I do not believe in capital punishment of any kind. My philosophy is this: we have no right to demean, diminish, or destroy a life. If they can't be rehabilitated, they should be incarcerated. But I was working in a system that says we're going to do it. It's not right for me to say how a man should die."

Chaplain McKee's successor, the Reverend Carroll L. Pickett, said that because the death penalty was in abeyance when he started to work at the Walls, he had no idea that walking men to their death would be among his responsibilities; his first walk into the death chamber was "extremely traumatic," he said, not least because the technique of killing by lethal injection had never been tried before. Over the years, Reverend Pickett has tried to make the process as humane as possible by devoting himself to comforting the condemned men and their families, honoring their final requests, and shortening the time each must lie strapped to the gurney before receiving his deadly dose.

I asked Reverend Pickett how he would feel if any of the men he escorted turned out to be innocent. He shook his head impatiently. "I can't deal in 'ifs,'" he said. "I don't look back at what the man did twelve years ago. I can't get involved in the legal stuff; I'm not a lawyer. My concern has to be that human being and what he needs that day."

The reverend may well be at peace about his role in the prison system, but physicians and rehabilitation specialists told me that TDC employees work under tremendously stressful and abusive conditions. Not only do many workers suffer from severe headaches, depression, and alcoholism; they also commonly inflict their pent-up aggression on their subordinates and spouses—many of whom suffer serious physical and emotional damage from this battering—and on their children, who in turn wreak havoc at school and are often rough with their peers. "It's pretty stressful," admitted Huntsville police detective Dave Collins, who quit his TDC job after four years spent guarding one of the toughest units at Ferguson, the prison for youthful offenders. "You see all kinds of garbage in there. A lot of [guards] let themselves get run over by the inmates; a lot can't take it and quit. Some of my family members noticed a change in me, said I'd become more cynical."

Sharon, a prison guard in her late forties who declined to give her last name, works the morning shift on death row. "It's not just tough, it's very depressing," she said. "There are not too many people who can do this—who can walk in and see someone who you know has killed somebody or raped a child, who's not been out in the free world for ten or fifteen years. You have to get very callous, feeding a guy that spits in your face and says, 'Yeah, and I'd kill *your* mother too.'"

Because Texas has no public-defender system, most death-row inmates are forced to rely on woefully incompetent, court-appointed counsel, and the churning of court-imposed execution dates and inmates' frantic appeals has meant that a number of inmates without any legal representation have come within minutes of being executed. Four death-row inmates in the last four years were found to be innocent and were released; at least four more have presented to the courts compelling claims of innocence. But their pleadings have been dismissed repeatedly because Texas law requires an inmate to produce new evidence of his innocence within thirty days of his conviction—an impossibly short time for a newly condemned person to procure trial transcripts (just preparing these often takes the court as long as thirty days), hire a new lawyer to reinvestigate the case, and file a motion for a new trial.

The thirty-day rule was upheld last year by the U.S. Supreme Court, much to the horror of Justice Harry A. Blackmun, who in his dissent warned his colleagues that "the execution of a person who can show that he is innocent comes perilously close to simple murder." The Court majority countered that those with technically inadmissible evidence can always fall back on executive clemency, "the 'fail-safe' in our criminal justice system." However, since 1976 not one appeal for clemency on the grounds of innocence has succeeded in Texas, where decisions are meted out by the governor and a parole board consisting of political appointees who follow no fixed set of procedures, are reluctant to second-guess the courts, and are accountable to no one.

As in many other death-penalty states, the dispensation of capital punishment in Texas is also tinged with racism. The disproportionate number of blacks on death row suggests that discriminatory practices continue to infect the state's police work, jury trials, and capital sentencing. Civil-rights groups have grown increasingly vocal on this issue. Meanwhile, violent crime continues, and frustrated white citizens, politicians, and law-enforcement officials have organized a slew of victims' rights groups that furiously condemn defense attorneys' "frivolous delaying tactics" and call for "justice now."

The debate and the high-stakes legal gambits for inmates' lives take place mostly in Austin, where a politically ambitious attorney general and a conservative legislature seem intent on maintaining and even expanding the death penalty; in Houston, which has the fourth-highest homicide rate of the nation's largest cities and thus has had seven times as many men executed as any other Texas jurisdiction; and as far away as Washington, where national anti-crime sentiment has inspired President Clinton to dream up fifty ways to expand the death penalty and the Supreme Court to progressively narrow death-row inmates' access to the federal courts.

But the eye of this storm is Huntsville, where the convicted killers wait. Life on "the row" has little to recommend it. Prisoners can choose to lift weights, work in the death-row garment factory, or pursue their appeals. Visitation rights are limited; the inmates are separated from all "free world" beings by bars and a narrow panel of thick glass laced with wire mesh. Those deemed security risks are chained inside metal cages when entertaining guests.

"Death row is the loneliest place in the world," said Lester Leroy Bower, a white, forty-six-year-old inmate who edits one of the row's two newspapers, attends Bible classes, and studies Hebrew and Greek. "You have people around you all the time, but you have very few friends. There is too much dying on the row, so you don't build really true bonds. And the hardest," added this husband and father of two teenage girls, his voice suddenly subdued, "is separation from family—never being able to touch 'em, hold 'em."

Death-penalty proponents have little pity for such talk from convicted murderers. Bower, however, insists he is innocent of the four murders for which he was sentenced to death in 1984 and says he has strong evidence pointing to four other suspects. Because of the thirty-day rule, however, no Texas court has agreed to hear his story.

Bower believes he was framed by corrupt law-enforcement officials allegedly involved in drug transactions with at least one of the murder victims. All of the evidence gathered against Bower was circumstantial; potentially exculpatory evidence mysteriously disappeared before the trial. Although within days of his conviction witnesses began coming forward with new evidence supporting Bower's innocence, his lawyer, off on a Mexican vacation, failed to meet the thirty-day deadline. Bower's harrowing trial experience, followed by a decade spent studying the cases of his neighbors on the row, has persuaded him that inside Texas's sometimes Kafkaesque criminal-justice system, one's innocence can have astonishingly little bearing on one's fate.

"You can convict almost anybody in Texas," he told me. "I'm white, fairly well educated, moderately articulate, have taken paralegal courses, and now I even have a good lawyer. That puts me a step up on a lot of people—and that has nothing to do with my innocence! Say I'm black, poor, uneducated, inarticulate, have no lawyer, have been put through the mill: I haven't got a chance."

Yet most Huntsville residents are sure that those executed in their town are guilty. "If they were innocent, it would've been found out way back then," insisted Diamond Kornegay, a retiree who, like many of Huntsville's relative newcomers, fled crime-ridden Houston for a peaceful life in the country. "Just look at all these lawyers, all these witnesses and everything!" Diamond, a chatty lady whose "daddy" was a cotton farmer and who grew up close to Huntsville, said the executions never bothered her.

"It's not a big deal to me. When I was a little bitty girl, they used to open up the Walls and take the schoolchildren through there. I saw the electric chair, but I never did think about it; I just put that out of my mind. If anyone ended up getting killed, well, they just did a bad thing, and that's the law."

It wasn't hard to see how such attitudes have been forged. Each morning, shrill whistles at 6:00 A.M., 7:00 A.M., and noon (denoting times for head-counting, work detail, and more head-counting) make it impossible for those within earshot to forget that their neighbor is a bureaucracy run on involuntary labor. The reminders continue all day long: trusties in their prison whites performing menial tasks, the changing of the guards in gray, prison vans trucking manacled inmates from unit to unit, and the startling profusion of wisecracking sheriffs and wardens who gather from all over Texas for seminars at Sam's prestigious Criminal Justice Institute and who stroll through town resplendent in starched jeans, smart cowboy hats, boots, and huge silver belt buckles.

Each weekday between 11:00 A.M. and 3:00 P.M., convicts from all over Texas are released at the Walls. For years their first stop was usually Bustin' Loose, a clothing store one block from the prison, where they could cash their release checks and pick up new clothes. But the state recently cut the stipend from $200 to $100, and since most new ex-cons are less willing to blow their few bucks, last fall the owners of Bustin' Loose were forced to close shop. But before they did, I met a burglar and a dope dealer there; both were in their twenties and both had trained to be bricklayers while inside (though neither seemed particularly interested in laying bricks now that he was free). By early afternoon both men, sporting new T-shirts and shorts, were stumbling down Twelfth Street, stone drunk.

Most ex-cons hightail it out of Huntsville within hours of being released, using the Greyhound vouchers the prison provides in their release packets. During my weeks in Huntsville I would occasionally stop by the Greyhound station to chat with the men as they waited for their buses to Houston or Dallas, Lubbock, Beaumont, or Port Arthur. Most releases I met were repeat offenders; almost all were Hispanic and black. An immensely unlikable murderer with a gold necklace and twisted grimace who had served only four years practically spat at me as he assured me that he had paid his debt to society. One, a large, drunken, white-haired black man, became quite chummy. He told me his name was Mr. Bum, or Mr. Wannabe, that he was "a bona fide Christian," that "prison is hell, emotionally, physically, intellectually, and don't let anybody tell you anything different," and that I was his kind of woman, baby. When he shook my hand good-bye, he tried to steal my ring.

On November 9, I learned that my turn had come and that I had been assigned to the media pool for the execution that night

of Anthony Cook, a white thirty-two-year-old construction worker from nearby Crockett who had abducted and murdered a
University of Texas law student in 1988. Cook was what is known
in the trade as "a volunteer," meaning that he had waived his
right to appeal and was ready to submit to his sentence, and it was
a pretty sure bet that his execution would proceed on schedule.
Until the last minute, attorney Elizabeth Cohen from the federally funded Texas Resource Center tried to persuade Cook to
change his mind, but he was not to be swayed. Cook believed that
he'd been saved by the Lord Jesus back in 1991 and that he was
headed straight for the right hand of God.

Cook spent his last day with his family, who Cohen said were
"not happy" about his decision and were "having a really hard
time." At 4:00 P.M. he was moved to the Walls' holding cell, and
after his double-meat-and-bacon cheeseburger, strawberry shake,
and shower, he and Cohen sat within yards of the death chamber
and talked about God.

"He's doing great, he can't wait," Cohen reported to me after-
ward. "He has no interest in changing his mind; he has more
interest in bringing me to Christianity. He keeps praying for me,
and he looks at me with tears in his eyes because I'm not saved."
After Cohen left, Cook visited with his closest spiritual advisers,
Baptist volunteer chaplains Jack and Irene Wilcox, who later told
me Cook begged them to "follow up on" Cohen's conversion after
his death.

Jack Wilcox had nothing but enthusiasm for the force of
Cook's conversion. "We walk into the death house, and he says to
me, 'Hey, Jack, I'm excited!' Two hours before he's going to die
and he's excited? I say, 'Fantastic! That's great!' . . . This man saw
prison five times, he committed a horrible kidnapping and murder . . . a sure loser!" exclaimed Jack, who himself had found the
Lord after a life on the streets. "And then three years later, you be
lookin' at a person prayin' to God."

"We would have liked to have seen him continue with his
appeals, because he was a great witness," Irene interrupted, "but
he believed in the death penalty."

Jack jumped back in, impatient. "It's not for us to say. A lot of
the men [on the row] are upset because he gave up his appeals. I
say, 'Look, the man's been prayin' to God for two years—you
don't get between a man and his prayers.' We wanna let God drive
the car," he explained, and then asked whether I had yet let the
Lord Jesus into my heart.

The evening of Cook's execution I attended a City Council meeting where neither the mayor, city manager, city councilmen, student body president, nor student-newspaper editor had any idea that Tony Cook had accepted with pleasure the state's invitation to be put to death later that night. Everyone came in talking about the day's big news: the Huntsville Hornets' star football coach was retiring after nineteen years. The main item on the City Council's agenda that evening was a hotly contested bid by Sam students and five bar owners to get drinking hours extended from midnight until 1:00 A.M. on weekdays and from 1:00 to 2:00 A.M. on Saturdays. The initiative lost by a wide margin—and not surprisingly: Huntsville is heavily Baptist and was dry until 1971. The students were up in arms at the outcome, and they stormed out of the meeting after threatening to unseat the councilmen in the upcoming January election (though only a few hundred Sam students ever bother to vote in local elections).

But I was thinking about that evening's execution. I'd never even seen anyone die, and here I was, about to witness a man's death, to observe it without objection. Already I felt sullied, voyeuristic. Yet this is the law, I told myself. What's more, this one should be easy: this man *wants* to die. And he did pump four bullets into that poor law student's head. I kept up this interior debate until it was time to report in at the TDC "Admin" building, just across from the Walls. I parked near the Dairy Queen and hurried through the foggy chill to the triple set of doors.

Several reporters had already gathered in the tiny Public Information Office. Two were chatting with assistant information director Brown about other executions they had attended; another, like me a first-time witness, was earnestly jotting down facts from his "Execution Information" briefing packet. Cook had requested no personal witnesses at his death, Brown told us; the family would not claim the body, which meant that Cook would be buried at state expense in the Colonel Joe Byrd Cemetery, named for the late assistant warden who not only supervised every execution from 1949 until his death in 1964 but also took it upon himself to tend the dead men's graves.

The phone rang at 11:56. Brown answered. "That's quick; they're ready to go," he said, getting up from his desk. We walked across the street to the Walls, some of us chatting, barely aware of a couple of protesters almost invisible in the fog. The Walls' handsome old clock face read 10:02. I wondered how many men had died inside the Walls since its clock last told the correct time.

Once we were inside the gates, an assistant warden led us across an interior courtyard with locked chain-link fences, down white corridors with white-tile floors, through one thick gray door after another, each opened with an enormous brass key. Brown was amazed by the different style of the new warden, Morris Jones, who was presiding tonight over his first execution. "I tell ya, this Jones, he's a new kind: quick, quick," he said. "No point in waiting, I guess."

We then were marched single file to the death house. The other woman reporter must have seen the fearful look in my eyes. She told me that she couldn't sleep for three nights after her first execution. "Just attend to the business at hand," she advised. As we sat waiting to be admitted into the witness room, Reverend Pickett walked Cook the dozen-odd steps from his tiny holding cell with its bright orange bars, past a shower and toilet, and into the antiseptic death chamber, where he would be strapped down onto the chrome gurney while the warden and reverend stood by. I asked public-information officer David Nunnelee whether it made any difference to him when the men whose death he witnessed were volunteers.

"I appreciate that they accept what they did and want to pay the penalty," he said, without hesitation. "You gotta respect that."

Defense attorney Owen subsequently disparaged this view. "Actually, Cook was the perfectly rehabilitated prisoner," Owen said, then mused about the fine theological line between the insanity plea of an inmate who claims to hear voices, and is therefore not competent to be executed, and a volunteer such as Cook, whose execution was expedited because he had heard the voice of Jesus promising him a heavenly escape from death row.

We got our signal and were abruptly herded into the carpeted witness room, along with two large wardens in khaki jackets and a small dark man in an even darker suit, who, I was told, was the one assistant attorney general who never talked to the press. We stood behind bars and a pane of thick glass, which separated us from the actual death chamber.

The view was stunning. Cook lay spread-eagled on the gurney, ready, bound by six thick leather straps. Although the press briefing listed his height as only five foot six, he looked enormous. His eyes were only partly open; his strong chin pointed upward. He was balding, and his longish auburn hair looked blond beneath the chilling fluorescent light. Ace bandages covered both hands and IVs were inserted into both forearms, his thin, short-sleeved prison shirt revealing a blurry tattoo. He wore blue, standard-issue prison garb and his own Etonic sneakers, purchased, I later learned, in the prison commissary for $21.75.

Near Cook's head stood Warden Jones; near Cook's feet stood Reverend Pickett, his hands folded. Suddenly I saw movement in front of me and realized that on Cook's far side was a one-way mirror in which we all were reflected. It was our own movement, not that of the symmetrical threesome in the death chamber itself, that had been captured in the glass. The effect was eerie; not only would I witness an execution but I would witness myself witnessing it. Behind the mirror, in an adjacent room, stood the executioner (whether man or woman, or more than one, no one would tell me), who would, upon a signal from the warden, activate the death device and introduce into Cook's veins the $71.50 fix consisting of what prison officials term "those substances necessary to cause death": sodium thiopental, which is the lethal component, pancuronium bromide, to relax and anesthetize, and potassium chloride, to stop the heartbeat.

"Do you have anything to say?" the warden muttered at 12:08. Cook opened his eyes.

"Yessir," he said, speaking into a big black microphone hung just over his head. "I just want to tell my family that I love them and I thank the Lord Jesus for giving me another chance and for saving me."

With that, Cook shut his eyes. The warden gave a small, sharp nod toward the person or persons behind the mirror. We all stood rigid, frozen. The silence was absolute, a perfect vacuum. Within seconds Cook took a sudden deep breath, gagged once, and stiffened his chin upward, all in one gesture. His chest expanded tremendously when he breathed, as if he had eagerly inhaled his own death. His arms were still outstretched and bound; his mouth and eyes were slightly open; nothing else moved.

My eyes slowly traced the contours of his body—the ninety degrees from his shiny bald crown to the end of his outstretched left arm, down the length of his pants leg, across the white sneakers, and up the near side—searching for signs of life, a cough, a twitch, a moan, a second thought. None came. I waited for him to exhale. But the air he had so urgently seized a moment before remained trapped in Cook's chest. The show was over; the passage from life to death was horrifyingly invisible, a silent and efficient erasure.

We waited. Finally, the warden called in Dr. Darrell Wells, a bearded emergency-room physician who attends most of the prison's executions. Wells checked Cook's eyes with a flashlight and his heart with a stethoscope. The play had ended. At 12:15, within five minutes of Anthony Cook's last gasp, the doctor pronounced him dead.

We filed out the way we came, more quickly this time, with little conversation. When I reached the Public Information Office, one of the reporters was already calling his bureau.

"Hi, Harry. He's history," he greeted his editor. Another reporter filed his story by modem while press officer Brown invited us all to the opening of a new 2,250-bed prison later that morning.

"Cold, ain't it?" a thin young guard greeted me as I walked back to my car. The clock at the Walls still read 10:02. A yellow traffic light flashed in front of the closed, eternally lit Dairy Queen. Cook's death made the 1:00 A.M. news on CNN, flickering in the nation's consciousness but an instant.

By 7:30 that morning at the Huntsville Funeral Home (which handles the bodies of all executed men), Tony Cook's mother, stepfather, brother, sister, assorted in-laws, cousins, and the Wilcoxes were paying their last respects to his open casket. Cook looked smaller than he had on the gurney; he had pretty, long eyelashes and delicate hands, a slightly cleft chin, and the shadow of a beard. He was dressed now in a blue oxford shirt with white stripes, and his mother stood over him, gently caressing his thin hair, his cheek, his ear. "He feels like you could just squeeze him back to life," she said. He had called her two hours before his death to tell her how excited he was about dying. "He certainly was at peace with hisself," she said.

"No more cages," sighed his sister as she touched her brother's chest, arms, face. "He's free, free, free!" She clutched his hand again and again, then finally kissed his forehead good-bye. I tried to fathom what it must feel like, after five years of no physical contact, to be allowed to touch a son or brother only after he is dead.

We followed the hearse through town to the muddy cemetery, where the six inmates who had prepared the grave were warming themselves over an ashcan fire. The seventeen family members clustered together, held one another, and cried, while Reverend Pickett read some prayers. Chaplain Jack Wilcox, in a hot-pink tie with a bright paisley print, said he'd never heard Tony say a bad word about anybody and read us a statement that Cook had written for the occasion: "Someday you will read in the papers that I have died—don't you believe a word of it . . ."

After the service Chaplain Wilcox pointed to one of the hundreds of crosses in the cemetery. "That's one of Tony's best friends, right there," he said. Since the markers have only prison numbers and no names, I asked how he knew. "I buried him," he said. "Last June." I later asked Reverend Pickett why the crosses have no names.

"It makes it more accurate," he told me. "We have many at the prison with the same name. There'll be another Tony Cook, but there'll never be another number like that number."

The air was dank and cold as I drove out of town, and I hoped the day's sharp rawness would clear my numbed senses. I headed north out to farm route 980, past sallow fields, unkempt trailer clusters, and the occasional satellite dish. Suddenly I saw, strung from a ragged barbed-wire fence, what looked like a wild dog or wolf, hanging upside down by its right rear foot. Its tail was splayed in a lazy S; its other legs were beautifully poised as if the animal had been caught in mid-leap by a photographer's lens.

I sped by, stopped, then backed up to make sure I wasn't hallucinating. The animal had been shot in the right shoulder, and bloody organs were dribbling out. So far only a single fly had discovered the catch; long-tailed, white-bellied birds took no notice as they hopped along the fence and pecked at the unmowed field.

Like somebody's trophy, the animal hung there, far more dignified than its surroundings. It was a coyote, I was later told, a predator. Nothing to feel sorry for, in other words: all cross-breeds were coyotes out here, and they ate the calves and young deer. It was hung there "as a warning to other coyotes," said one veteran hunter; another suggested it was hung "to let other farmers know they're doin' their part" in keeping the coyote population down. "That's just kinda the old way here in Texas," a former state game warden told me. Another old-timer, a man who'd mounted the rear end of a deer on the wall of his tiny living room wall, gave one more reason: "Somebody wants to show off that he killed somethin'," he said, then broke into a toothless grin.

All these explanations somehow made sense. But I wondered why I was so transfixed by this roadside display of a predator's comeuppance. Something about the crude, fresh death jarred me in a way that Cook's execution had not. That meticulous choreography had anesthetized me to the reality that a man was being killed before my eyes. But the flesh and blood of this handsome, dripping creature made both its death and its outlaw status immediately palpable.

From what I'd read about the stench of electrocution and the vividness of public hangings, I imagined that witnessing deaths by these means would have an immediacy that would preclude numbness. The lethal-injection method, first used in Texas in 1982 and now adopted by most death-penalty states as more humane, has turned dying into a still life, thereby enabling the state to kill without anyone involved feeling anything at all.

I wondered how viewing such a non-event could satisfy the desire for retribution so often expressed by death-penalty advocates and the families of victims. I wondered whether Huntsville's sterile, bloodless executions of the last twelve years might partly account for residents' wholesale disinterest and denial that what went on deep inside the Walls might have anything to do with them.

But it's not just here in Huntsville; we are all inured to such smooth exterminations. Any remaining glimmers of doubt—about whether the man received due process, about his guilt, about our right to take a life—cause us to rationalize these deaths with such catchwords as "heinous," "deserved," "deterrent," "justice," and "painless." We have perfected the art of institutional killing to the degree that it has deadened our natural, quintessentially human response to death.

When I returned to town, a student activist was waiting at my hotel to let me know how upset he and his colleagues were by the City Council's refusal to extend legal drinking hours. Outside my window, Sam cheerleaders feverishly waved their pink banners in practice for Saturday's game. A TDC official phoned to tell me not to bother to show up the following night for Dorsie Johnson's execution: he'd just gotten stayed until January.

Feeling hungry, I decided to check out Mr. Hamburger, Huntsville's original fast-food shack, which since it went up in the Fifties has stood a block west of the Walls. A now-faded sandwich board out front reads, TRY OUR KILLER BURGERS.

So I tried one: "Double meat, double cheese, lettuce, tomato, mustard, mayonnaise, pickle, and jalapeños," explained Willie Mae Jenkins, a pretty short-order cook with a monogrammed gold tooth who has been serving up Killer and Jr. Killer Burgers for eighteen years.

"So why's it called a Killer Burger?" I asked.

Willie Mae smiled, apparently surprised by the question and a little embarrassed at not having a ready answer. "I really don't know," she said. "I think it has something to do with the jalapeños."

IV. THE CLINTON CRIME BILL/SEEKING SOLUTIONS

EDITOR'S INTRODUCTION

The final section of this compilation begins with an excerpt from the 1994 State of the Union address of President Bill Clinton, which describes his intentions in putting together "the toughest crime bill in history." A notable feature of the bill is its [previously discussed] "three strikes and you are out" provision. It also calls for the addition of as many as 100,000 police officers around the nation to provide more community policing, curtailment of firearms beyond the very limited provisions of the Brady Bill, boot camps for youthful offenders, and money for drug treatment. After a fierce battle in congress in which youth programs were assailed by the Republican opposition as "pork," the bill passed into law. In keeping with the political climate of the time, the bill has strongly conservative elements. Among these are the addition of fifty new offenses punishable by death and provisions making appeal access to the higher courts more difficult.

In a related piece from *U. S. News & World Report*, Ted Gest and Gordon Witkin wonder if Clinton's crime bill can accomplish as much as it claims. The bill provides more funding for the states, but only if they adhere to "truth in sentencing" rules that sharply cut the disparity between sentence time and actual time served. Yet, the authors point out, in states that already employ "truth in sentencing," the rate of violent crime has continued to increase. Harsher sentences do not mean that criminals will believe they will actually be caught and therefore be deterred from committing more crimes. Also, the addition of more police in the crime bill has conditions attached that steadily shift financing to the cities—conditions that may make the financially-squeezed municipalities balk. But according to the authors even if police presence is beefed up, no correlation has yet been shown to exist between police strength and crime rates.

An article from *The Humanist* in which its co-editor Rick Szykowny interviews Jerome Miller, a criminal justice specialist, examines another aspect of criminal sentencing: the situation of young black males. According to Miller, blacks make up over 50 percent of the U.S. prison population, with whites adding another 30 percent or more, and Hispanics 15–17 percent. As this trend continues, Miller comments, a majority of young black men will be in prison by the turn of the century, by which time, Miller theorizes, we will have a prison population of 7.5 million people, of which 4 million will be black. Miller has a startling vision of the future, with an increasingly powerful, gulag-like system of camps and prisons across the country.

The final article, "The Economics of Crime," taken from *BusinessWeek*, focuses on the overall cost of crime. According to the authors, Michael Mandel and Paul Magnusson, Americans spend about $425 billion each year—both directly and indirectly—on crime. The authors discuss economically sound and practical solutions to the growing problem of crime in the United States.

STATE OF THE UNION[1]

. . . But while Americans are more secure from threats abroad, I think we all know that in many ways we are less secure from threats here at home. Every day the national peace is shattered by crime. In Petaluma, Calif., an innocent slumber party gives way to agonizing tragedy for the family of Polly Klaas. An ordinary train ride on Long Island [New York] ends in a hail of 9-millimeter rounds. A tourist in Florida is nearly burned alive by bigots simply because he is black. Right here in our nation's capital a brave young man named Jason White, a policeman, the son and grandson of policemen, is ruthlessly gunned down.

Violent crime and the fear it provokes are crippling our society, limiting personal freedom and fraying the ties that bind us. The crime bill before Congress gives you a chance to do something about it, a chance to be tough and smart.

What does that mean? Let me begin by saying I care a lot about this issue. Many years ago when I started out in public life I was the Attorney General of my state. I served as the Governor

[1] Excerpt from a speech by William J. Clinton from *Vital Speeches of the Day* F. 15, '94. Copyright © 1994 by Vital Speeches of the Day. Reprinted by permission.

for a dozen years. I know what it's like to sign laws increasing penalties, to build more prison cells, to carry out the death penalty. I understand this issue. And it is not a simple thing.

First, we must recognize that most violent crimes are committed by a small percentage of criminals, who too often break the laws even when they're on parole. Now those who commit crimes should be punished. And those who commit repeated violent crimes should be told when you commit a third violent crime you will be put away and put away for good. Three strikes, and you are out.

Second, we must take serious steps to reduce violence and prevent crime beginning with more police officers and more community policing. We know—we know right now that police who work the streets, know the folks, have the respect of the neighborhood kids, focus on high crime areas—we know that they are more likely to prevent crime as well as catch criminals. Look at the experience of Houston, where the crime rate dropped 17 percent in one year when that approach was taken.

Here tonight is one of those community policemen, a brave young detective, Kevin Jett, whose beat is eight square blocks in one of the toughest neighborhoods in New York. Every day he restores some sanity and safety, and a sense of values and connection to the people whose lives he protects. I'd like to ask him to stand up and be recognized tonight. Thank you, sir.

You will be given a chance to give the children of this country, the law-abiding working people of this country—and don't forget, in the toughest neighborhoods in this country, in the highest-crime neighborhoods in this country, the vast majority of people get up every day and obey the law, pay their taxes, do their best to raise their kids—they deserve people like Kevin Jett. And you're going to be given a chance to give the American people another one hundred thousand of them, well-trained, and I urge you to do it.

You have before you crime legislation which also establishes a police corps to encourage young people to get an education, pay it off by serving as police officers, which encourages retiring military personnel to move into police forces, an inordinate resource for our country. One which has a safe-schools provision which will give our young people the chance to walk to school in safety and to be in school in safety instead of dodging bullets. These are important things.

The third thing we have to do is to build on the Brady bill, the

Brady law. To take further steps—to take further steps to keep guns out of the hands of criminals.

I want to say something about this issue. Hunters must always be free to hunt. Law-abiding adults should always be free to own guns and protect their homes. I respect that part of our culture; I grew up in it.

But I want to ask the sportsmen and others who lawfully own guns to join us in this campaign to reduce gun violence. I say to you: I know you didn't create this problem, but we need your help to solve it. There is no sporting purpose on earth that should stop the United States Congress from banishing assault weapons that out-gun police and cut down children.

Fourth, we must remember that drugs are a factor in an enormous percentage of crimes. Recent studies indicate, sadly, that drug use is on the rise again among our young people. The crime bill contains—all the crime bills contain more money for drug treatment for criminal addicts and boot camps for youthful offenders, that include incentives to get off drugs and to stay off drugs.

Our Administration's budget, with all its cuts, contains a large increase in funding for drug treatment and drug education. You must pass them both; we need them desperately.

My fellow Americans, the problem of violence is an American problem. It has no partisan or philosophical element. Therefore, I urge you to find ways as quickly as possible to set aside partisan differences and pass a strong, smart, tough crime bill.

But further, I urge you to consider this: as you demand tougher penalties for those who choose violence, let us also remember how we came to this sad point. In our toughest neighborhoods, on our meanest streets, in our poorest rural areas, we have seen a stunning and simultaneous breakdown of community, family and work—the heart and soul of civilized society.

This has created a vast vacuum which has been filled by violence and drugs and gangs. So I ask you to remember that even as we say no to crime, we must give people, especially our young people, something to say yes to.

Many of our initiatives from job training, to welfare reform, to health care, to national service will help to rebuild distressed communities, to strengthen families, to provide work. But more needs to be done. That's what our community empowerment agenda is all about, challenging businesses to provide more investment through empowerment zones; insuring banks will make loans in the same communities their deposits come from; passing legislation to unleash the power of capital through community development banks to create jobs; opportunity and hope where they're needed most.

But I think you know that to really solve this problem we'll all have to put our heads together, leave our ideological armor aside and find some new ideas to do even more. And let's be honest, we all know something else, too. Our problems go way beyond the reach of government. They're rooted in the loss of values, in the disappearance of work and the breakdown of our families and our communities.

My fellow Americans, we can cut the deficit, create jobs, promote democracy around the world, pass welfare reform and health care, pass the toughest crime bill in history and still leave too many of our people behind. The American people have got to want to change from within if we're going to bring back work and family and community. . . .

A COLD-EYED LOOK AT CRIME[2]

Their constituents jittery and their re-elections far from assured, key members of Congress sat down last week to write the most expensive anticrime law ever. They began haggling over details of a bill that could provide $30 billion to states and localities for police protection, imprisonment, and crime prevention. They also faced the emotional issues of guns and race. Pro-gun forces opposed a ban on 19 types of "assault weapons." And prosecutors battled a "racial justice" provision that they complained could bring executions to a halt; advocates said the measure would enable defendants to challenge racial bias in the death penalty.

With prospects shaky for enacting health care and welfare reform this election year, Congress was under pressure to act on a significant domestic-policy issue. Still, the crime bill could run into a number of pitfalls. *U.S. News* examined the two initiatives virtually certain to pass and to consume a majority of the measure's spending: prisons and police.

---

[2] Article by Ted Gest and Gordon Witkin from *U.S. News & World Report* Je. 27, '94. Copyright © 1994 by U.S. News & World Report. Reprinted by permission.

"Truth in sentencing"
Longer terms may not cut crime

The horror stories about crimes committed by felons released from prison never end. Often, the criminal has served only a fraction of his term. "Judges pretend that defendants will get long sentences, and they get out the back door," says James Wootton of the Safe Streets Alliance, a Washington, D.C.-based group lobbying for a get-tough crime bill. "That's what drives people crazy."

The prison population leapt from 330,000 in 1980 to a projected one million plus this year, but congressional crime fighters want states to crack down harder. They will set aside billions of dollars—Republicans demand more than $10 billion—to help states build new lockups. But there's a catch: states must enact "truth in sentencing" rules that sharply cut the disparity between sentences and time served. Advocates believe convicts should serve at least 85 percent of their time. Murderers serve an average of only five and one-half years, complains North Dakota Senator Kent Conrad, whose wife was assaulted near the Capitol by a convict who had served only one fourth of a term for rape.

Such a provision would put the federal government behind a trend that is already gaining ground in the states. Missouri enacted an 85 percent rule last month, and the Michigan Senate last week passed a version that would replace "good time" credits to well-behaved inmates with extra "bad time" for those misbehaving behind the walls.

Resolving the sentencing mess would quell a big public complaint, but it may have little impact on crime. Consider Delaware. Starting in 1990, it required convicts to serve 75 percent of their terms. Earlier, "we had to tell victims that their assailant might get out after six months of a five-year sentence," says Attorney General Charles Oberly. "Now, we can look them in the eye and say they will serve three and one-half to four years."

But Delaware's coffers are so bare that the overhaul amounted to a trade-off: more lockup time for violent criminals and less for nonviolent convicts like burglars. By that standard, the plan has worked. Three fourths of Delaware's inmates today have been convicted of violent crimes, up 10 percent since the state began reforming sentencing in 1987. But the violent crime rate increased dramatically at the same time, from 430 to 726 for every one hundred thousand residents. Truth in sentencing "doesn't mean that crime will drop tomorrow or next year," admits Judge Richard Gebelein of Wilmington, head of a panel overseeing the sentencing system. Even if they know punishment is harsher, the next generation of lawbreakers may be undeterred, partly because they have little fear of being caught. And when some repeat offenders do more time, truth in sentencing delays their release but does not prevent it. So, those bent on crime will still take their toll.

The federal government and many states are trying to plug that gap with "three strikes and you're out" laws that would incarcerate three-time violent felons for life. Congress will decide soon on details for federal crimes, but more prison construction is inevitable. "Three strikes" is bound to prevent some crimes, yet the cost is steep. In New York State, which has more than doubled its prison beds in a decade, Assembly Speaker Sheldon Silver asks, "Do people feel safer? The answer in New York and elsewhere in the nation is a resounding no."

Cops with strings attached
A lesser deterrent than meets the eye

Early last fall, St. Petersburg, Fla., Police Chief Darrel Stephens took a look at a new $150 million federal program to help strapped locales hire new cops—and recommended that his city take a pass. The strings attached were too cumbersome, the funding requirements too burdensome, the benefits too modest, Stephens told Mayor David Fischer. But Fischer overruled his chief. Not pursuing the money, the mayor reasoned, might send a message of complacency, and so St. Petersburg applied for the funds.

That same ambivalence is now evident on a wider scale, because President Clinton's plan to add one hundred thousand cops to the nation's streets is a key plank of the crime bill. The money for St. Petersburg was only a modest precursor of the $9 billion, six-year federal program likely to emerge from Congress.

Adding one hundred thousand cops would represent an almost 17 percent increase in the nearly 603,000 full-time law enforcement officers nationwide, and polls show the public strongly supports the idea. But as the plan has come into sharper focus, mayors, police chiefs and criminologists are wondering whether there may be less there than meets the eye.

For starters, one hundred thousand cops are not as many nor as visible as they might seem. Each officer works 40 hours, but a week has 168 hours. Add time for illness, vacation, and training, and it takes about five and a half officers to staff one position round the clock throughout the year. The political imperative to spread the wealth could also dilute the impact. The $150 million precursor program has awarded money to 250 jurisdictions in all 50 states, providing 2,023 additional cops. That yielded anywhere from one officer in Hayneville, Ala., to 54 in Los Angeles.

Many of them may not hit the streets for months. San Antonio was awarded a $3 million hiring supplement grant last December [1993] for 40 new officers. They began six months of training in March; they won't be available for full deployment until next January [1995].

Some fear the larger forces could overwhelm the rest of the system. In Fresno, Calif., last year [1993], officials warned that a proposed expansion of the police force from 420 to 520 would result in new arrests costing $10 million a year to process. The city agreed to add only 47 officers.

Many cities have such severe money problems that they may not even be able to apply for new cops. The crime bill will likely require cities to pay 25 percent of police costs in the first year, then take over a bigger share each year, shouldering the entire burden after five years. Local officials grumble that they also will get stuck with ancillary expenses for training and equipment like guns. Planners in San Antonio say they'll have to spend $3.98 million from the city's general fund for such items over the three-year life of a $3 million federal grant.

Mayors and police chiefs are also concerned that the new cops must be part of a plan to embrace "community policing"—a strategy emphasizing interaction with neighborhood residents to solve problems. "What happens to good, healthy departments that don't subscribe to this theory?" asks Dan Rosenblatt of the International Association of Chiefs of Police. Local authorities would like the freedom to use the money more flexibly than currently envisioned—for technology or support personnel, if that is the biggest need—instead of being forced to use most of it for new officers.

When the local grousing grew noisy earlier this spring, exasperated Clinton administration officials fired back. Quit whining, they said: community policing is a necessary change in the culture of policing. Federal officials noted, too, that the legislation will allow the attorney general to waive matching-fund requirements for truly strapped cities and pointed out that about 15 percent of the money would be available for ancillary items like equipment. "But 'flexibility' is a bit of a euphemism for saying, 'We want the federal government to pay the whole bill.' And the answer to that is, 'No,'" adds a Justice Department official. Given the president's "unprecedented" commitment to the idea, the official said, "I don't think it's at all unreasonable to say, 'You [cities] all are going to have to dig into your pockets, too.'"

And many will, despite landmark research in Kansas City, Mo., in the 1970s that showed no correlation between police strength and crime rates. That hasn't stopped Kansas City Chief Steven Bishop from applying for federal money. "We must clearly articulate that more police does not equal less crime," he says. "But adding more police officers is an absolute necessity for community policing. Violent crime has escalated beyond our ability to respond."

NO JUSTICE, NO PEACE: AN INTERVIEW WITH JEROME MILLER[3]

According to the latest (what else?) polls, the fear of crime has become a full-scale national panic: over one-quarter of the respondents—28 percent—in a recent *Washington Post*/ABC News poll cited crime and drugs as the greatest problems facing the nation, leaving in the dust such previous winners as unemployment (9 percent), health care (8 percent), and foreign policy (2 percent).

This explosion of fear—unreasoning, all-consuming, and markedly anti-humanistic—is tearing away at our national sanity and poses an ugly threat to our future. Consider some recent events: in October 1993, the mayor of Washington, D.C., Sharon Pratt Kelly, formally asked President Clinton to send the National Guard into the city to help "secure" black neighborhoods. Although the District of Columbia is the most heavily policed sector of the nation, it has also (not coincidentally) become the nation's "murder capital": 1,300 homicides in three years. Some members of Congress have even demanded that the Justice Department

---

[3] Article by Rick Szykowny from *The Humanist* Ja./F. '94. Copyright © 1994 by The Humanist. Reprinted by permission.

deputize them as U.S. marshals and allow them to carry hand-guns. Orrin "Quick Draw" Hatch and other congressional personnel have already been armed and deputized.

While some people are justly concerned about the implications of placing the nation's capital under military occupation, others have enthusiastically embraced such initiatives. For example, in a recent appearance on *Charlie Rose*, jazz critic and self-acclaimed "hanging judge" Stanley Crouch called for the U.S. military to operate internment camps within U.S. borders for our "internal enemies." And in Puerto Rico, a commonwealth of the United States, hundreds of National Guardsmen and police have taken over 23 public-housing projects since June, usually (as Dave Beard of the Associated Press describes it) "in swift nighttime operations complete with helicopters, armored personnel carriers, and shouted orders to residents."

Meanwhile, in New York City, a man shoots and kills two muggers who attempt to hold him up as he walks home. Much of the city responds to the deaths of these two black teenagers with barely concealed rejoicing. "They miscalculated when they tried to pick on him," said one citizen, who sent the man a $500 prize, "and I'm glad they did it." Another man told reporters: "I wish he took out a few more of them." Two days later, two off-duty police officers separately shot and killed two more alleged muggers.

And yet, in the latest issue of *The Public Interest* quarterly, Jeffrey Snyder insists that we have become "a nation of cowards and shirkers" and that the only feasible solution to crime would be to *arm everyone.*

What is happening in this country? We asked Jerome Miller, the executive director of the National Center for Institutions and Alternatives. The NCIA, headquartered in Alexandria, Virginia, has worked hard to develop a range of humane alternatives to our current strategies of incarceration and retribution, while Miller himself is among the most thoughtful and progressive analysts of American crime policy. Not surprisingly, he had much to say about the hidden agenda of our malfunctioning and brutal criminal-justice system.

The Humanist interviewed Miller on October 21, 1993.

The Humanist: Tell me about the National Center for Institutions and Alternatives. What kind of work does it do?

Miller: Well, we're a nonprofit group that I founded about 15 years ago now, to provide some alternative ways of looking at the criminal-justice system. We do a lot of alternative sentencing for people who would otherwise go to prison or jail. We do a lot of work with street offenders and with some white-collar offenders as well. We do a fair amount of death-penalty work, preparing mitigative studies for people being tried on capital offenses. We do research on various issues. We also do some consulting with reference to prison and jail overcrowding, and then we have an active clinical program for violent offenders of various sorts.

The Humanist: When you say you do "alternative sentencing," does that mean you're working with various law-enforcement authorities and prison systems?

Miller: No, primarily with individual cases. We've probably done 12,000 to 15,000 alternative sentencing proposals, which means we go into court on the day of sentencing and propose a range of options for people who would otherwise be institutionalized.

The Humanist: What kind of options?

Miller: Oh, a wide range of things: community service; restitution to the victim; if necessary, various forms of supervision within the community; drug or alcohol treatment programs. We try to do for the average offender what a thinking, compassionate, middle-class parent or brother or son would do for someone in their family were they in trouble—that is, design some kind of program that would hopefully prevent the person from committing any more crimes, but also that would try to deal with that person decently and humanely. And we try, as much as possible, to divert them from the criminal-justice system, and certainly from the correctional system, which we see as ultimately much more destructive than helpful.

The Humanist: How big is the NCIA?

Miller: We have a staff of around two hundred. Some of them are in direct programs, like the closed facility for violent youngsters we run down in Florida—kids committed to us primarily on charges of murder and serious aggravated assault and that sort of thing. We also run a fairly large program in Baltimore for mentally retarded offenders who otherwise would be in the back wards of state hospitals; we have them in a variety of supervised living arrangements in apartments around the Baltimore area. Then our central office in Alexandria, Virginia, does mostly alternative sentencing. And we have a clinical program that deals with violent offenders and sex offenders; we always have about 60 or so people getting treatment in that program on any given day.

The Humanist: So your operations span pretty much the entire United States?

Miller: Yes, we've had offices in a number of states, although we had to pull back because it just got to be too much to manage. Some of those offices have spun off on their own. The offices in New York City, San Francisco, and Chicago are separate entities now, locally incorporated.

The Humanist: And how did you end up in this field?

Miller: Well, I'd previously headed a number of state systems. I was the head of the Pennsylvania Youth Correction system for Governor Milton Shapp, and when he left office I decided to found this organization. Before that, I headed the Illinois Department of Children and Family Services; and before that I was on the cabinet of Governor Frank Sargent, a Republican governor of Massachusetts, and headed the youth-correction system there.

The Humanist: And how would you describe the success of the NCIA's programs? What kind of results are you getting?

Miller: Well, most of the studies done on our alternative sentencing have been very positive. I think we can mitigate a lot of recidivism and cut back on serious offending, and we can certainly break into the cycle of violence which so much characterizes the present corrections and criminal-justice system in this country—which is now probably the single greatest threat to our national well-being in our history. The single greatest contributor to crime and mayhem on the streets today is the criminal-justice system itself.

The Humanist: Then what do you think the purpose or philosophy of criminal justice is, or should be? What kind of purpose animates you?

Miller: Well, hopefully to bring some peace and calm to the community—but I don't think that is true any longer. There's been a real sea change in this country in our approach to criminal justice. For the most part, particularly in the last six to eight years, our "war on crime" has been focused on the poor and minorities, especially black men. It hasn't come back yet to bite the majority—but that will ultimately happen. I don't recall seeing anything like this ever before. And you know, I was a psychiatric social-work officer in the Air Force for ten years, with the Strategic Air Command and with the Tactical Air Command in this country and overseas, so I don't come from a tremendously liberal background. But I've been around the criminal-justice field some 30 years now, and I've never seen anything like what we've been seeing in the last decade, much of it coming out of the so-called war on drugs. It's now routine for prosecutors to engage in the worst kinds of dissembling and dishonesty, for the police to lie and subvert the truth in pursuit of a confession, to pay snitches, and to subvert justice in every way without a single pang of conscience or second thought about it.

The Humanist: You're saying this happens now *more* than it has in the past?

Miller: Oh, much more. I mean, there was probably much more open police brutality in the 1930s in terms of extracting confessions and so on, but it's a much more powerful *establishment* now. It's a huge, multibillion-dollar industry, and it has become very subversive of American democratic principles. I think the majority of the white population gets a little inkling here and there with things like the Waco tragedy or even the Randy Weaver siege out in Utah. These incidents give you some idea of what's going on in terms of the gross misuse of power by the police, by prosecutors, by the courts, really with little regard for truth and less regard for anything decent or humane. This establishment has just built itself up fantastically over the last decade. And its power has mostly been concentrated on the black community. I've just written a book which has been accepted by Cambridge University Press, to be published early next year; it will be entitled *Search and Destroy: On the Plight of the African-American Male in the American Criminal-Justice System*. And I predict in it—much in line with what Norwegian criminologist Nils Christie has said—that, by the turn of the century, we will have the absolute majority of young black men in the correctional system on any given day, most of them in camps and in prisons around the country. Certainly every indication is that we're going in that direction, and I don't see any great shift in the Clinton administration away from it.

The Humanist: That brings up an interesting point, because in our last issue our "Civil Liberties Watch" columnist, Barbara Dority, wrote a piece on the state of American prisons, and she said: "It's now official: it's cheaper to send a person to Harvard" than to prison.

Miller: Oh, there's no question of that.

The Humanist: But why is that? I think most people would look at that statistic and find it absolutely incredible.

Miller: Well, it's a very expensive, unaccountable bureaucracy. There's no more unaccountable system than a corrections system; the clientele consists of convicted criminals, so it would be virtually unpatriotic to respond to their needs. It's also a very, very expensive system to run, just in terms of the bureaucracy. I be-

lieve the average cost is actually somewhere around $20,000 to
$30,000 per year. If you look at the juvenile system, which is
worse, and where in many states now you'll find almost exclusively black kids—at least in the state institutions—it's costing
between $60,000 to $70,000 per year, per kid, literally to destroy
them. We're not talking about anything good happening to them
in these places.

The Humanist: But if you turn to a magazine like *Newsweek,* or if
you turn on the nightly news, you'll never see that issue raised,
and you'll never see the discussion framed in those kind of racial
terms.

Miller: That's because it's in code. I read an op-ed piece in the
New York Times by Lani Guinier, in which she referred to the
"rhetorical wink." There are certain code words that allow you
never to have to say *race,* but everybody knows that's what you
mean—and *crime* is one of those rhetorical winks. So when we talk
about locking up more and more people, what we're really talking
about is locking up more and more black men. That's what everyone means, that's certainly what's driving the New York City may-
oral election at this point, and you can see it happening all over
the country. You're not supposed to mention race, of course, and
if you do you're being divisive, but that's what it's all about.

The Humanist: The corporate media usually frames the debate
over the criminal-justice system as follows: you have conservatives, on the one hand, saying that the criminal-justice system
should be in the business of punishment; and you have the
"bleeding-heart liberals," on the other, saying that it should be
about rehabilitation. But what would you say? Is it about either?
Is it about both?

Miller: Well, I don't think all that many liberals talk about rehabilitation any more. I notice Lee Brown did a bit in his new drug
policy proposal, and certainly Janet Reno does to a degree, but I
doubt there's much commitment to that. There was a myth circu-
lated very successfully in the early years of the Reagan administration that rehabilitation doesn't work, that there was no evidence to prove that any of the rehabilitative programs had ever
worked. As I say, it was a myth, and it was put forth by a New York
City sociologist named Robert Martinson, whom I knew quite well
personally and who tragically killed himself in later years. It was
very interesting, because Bob was basically a kind of Trotskyite,
and his earlier writings on this advanced the conclusion that we
should actually begin closing prisons down. But the myth was

taken up by the right, particularly by neoconservatives like James Q. Wilson and others of the ilk, and it was used to justify a theory of "incapacitation" which said that, since rehabilitation doesn't work, let's just lock them up. The Rand Corporation was the first to develop the theory of incapacitation. Its people came out of the Defense Department after having done all their successful work in Vietnam and presented themselves as experts in criminal justice. They pretty much called the shots in those years.

The Humanist: Which years are these?

Miller: This was in the late 1970s, and then they really got into things in the 1980s. Wilson first spoke about these issues in *Thinking About Crime,* a book that rallied conservatives around this issue in the mid-1970s and succeeded in moving this country toward this model of deterrence and incapacitation as the only justification for the corrections system. From there, we moved to mandatory sentences and "do the crime, do the time" type rhetoric. What was *not* said, however, although this has clearly been the case—as they say, it was a rhetorical wink—was that this policy was meant to apply primarily to minorities. That was never talked about. Wilson later wrote a book with Richard Herrnstein, the Harvard psychologist, on crime and human nature, in which they hinted—another rhetorical wink—that crime may, in fact, be genetic; the wink being that it's probably black. That book was well received by liberal commentators.

The Humanist: Certainly crime has become the most racially divisive issue for American society today. I watched your appearance on C-SPAN, and I remember the woman from Florida who called in to say: "I know you're not going to want to hear this, but nine out of 10 people who are committing violent crimes are from the inner city. They are black . . . and nobody wants to face this problem. It's totally and completely out of hand, and it's a segment of our society that we better do something about."

Miller: Yes—"lock them away." Of course, the genetic arguments put forth by people like Wilson get everyone else off the hook. His earlier book openly disparaged the idea of root causes of crime. It was silly even to think about them; we just needed to stop crime. Then, in his later book, he talked about these genetic components, and certainly that is a big element even of his latest book on the "moral sense"—that somehow we inherit a certain moral sense, I guess the implication being that some races inherit more than others. It's a bizarre sort of thing, but I think much of the liberal community is open to that sort of reasoning these days.

We've turned away from looking at the social factors and social issues that create crime.

We don't want to talk about things like adequate income, employment, anti-poverty programs—all of that is now passé. And so we're left with the idea that criminals therefore must somehow or other be simply wicked persons, quite unlike the rest of us— and if we can genetically define them, that makes it even easier. It's an easy way out. Then one doesn't have to feel any guilt for what goes on in one's society.

I'm very pessimistic about where things are heading. We're now close to a million people in prison, and if you include the jails, we'll soon reach 1.5 million. Somewhere around 1984 or 1985 we reached the point where the absolute majority of men in our prisons and jails were minorities, mostly black. Depending on whose statistics you look at—it's certainly been my impression— over 50 percent of the people in prison now are black. If you include Hispanics (some of whom are black), it adds another 15 to 17 percent, while slightly over 30 percent are white. So we're at a point now where over two-thirds of our prison populations are nonwhite minorities. That's the first time in our history that this has ever been the case. If you look back to the 1920s, when the black population in the country was approximately the same as it is now—it was about 11 percent then, it's about 12 percent now— only about 20 percent of federal and state inmates were black. But now we're well over 50 percent. I think that fact, in itself, has changed the quality of the discussion. Because now when we talk about building more prisons, when we talk about longer sentences, when we talk about throwing away the keys, when we talk about cracking down on violent offenders, everyone knows that we're talking about blacks. And so the sky is the limit now.

The Humanist: Has the NCIA done any kind of breakdown on "black" crime versus "white" crime?

Miller: Oh, sure.

The Humanist: The majority of crimes in this country are still committed by whites, correct?

Miller: Oh, sure, including the majority of violent crimes. There is no question of that. And there is no question as well that there is more violent crime in the inner city; that has always been the case. But there were more murders in one year in San Francisco in the late 1800s, when it had a population of around 30,000 to 35,000 people, than there were in the late 1980s, when San Francisco had a population of 700,000.

The Humanist: Then why do Americans today believe that they are experiencing some unprecedented epidemic of violence and crime?

Miller: There's just very little sense of history about this. They talk about the L.A. riots, for example, as being the worst in our history. Of course, that's total nonsense. If you look at the Detroit riots, if you look at the draft riots in New York City in the mid-1800s, the death toll was much higher and the destruction much greater than anything that occurred in Los Angeles. But there's very little sense of history, and there's very little desire to look at these things with some sort of perspective. The homicide rate for black men, for example, was higher in the early 1930s than it was throughout most of the 1980s and 1990s—only in the late 1960s, 1972, 1981, and 1991 did it reach the levels that it had in 1934. But this fact is widely ignored, even by people like Daniel Patrick Moynihan, who talks constantly about the bucolic, halcyon days of the 1930s and 1940s. Now, to some degree he's correct—there were ethnic neighborhoods back then that obviously were a great deal safer and a lot less disorganized. But violence within the black community was generally ignored in the 1920s and 1930s, and so were the very high rates of violent crime that occurred after Reconstruction—most of it white-on-black violence.

Now, there is no question that you're at much greater risk walking around a poor neighborhood at midnight in Washington, D.C., than you would be in some rural town out in Iowa. The question is whether or not we're going to *do something* to begin to address the causes of such an environment. And it's now our belief that a significant percentage of the violence in our cities is being created by the criminal-justice system itself. I would use the District of Columbia as a prime example. It is now (the last I heard) the murder capital of the United States for cities with populations over 100,000. The District of Columbia is also the incarceration capital of the nation, and has been for quite some time. It incarcerates somewhere around 2,400 people per 100,000 now; I believe the national average is a little over 200 per 100,000. Even for most cities, the District of Columbia incarcerates at much higher rates than usual, both juveniles and adults. And I think what they've succeeded in doing is to create this huge alumni association on the streets for people who have been run through D.C.'s reform schools, jails, and prisons. It's almost a rite of passage for a young black male teenager to be arrested, to be handcuffed (often to peers) and dragged off in police vans, to be mug-shot, to sit in jail until released—most of it, incidentally, for nothing approaching violent crime, most of it for very small-time stuff. This policy carries with it a large number of very serious, unanticipated consequences. I think as a result they've re-created the culture of prison on the street. You really aren't anyone on the street unless you've done time in prison or in jail or in the detention center. The violent subculture of prison now permeates the streets, and that is a direct result of this overreliance on incarceration. And when you add to it law-enforcement techniques that are overtly and actively destructive of even minimal social cohesion within the community, then you have a major problem.

The Humanist: What are examples of those techniques?

Miller: Well, for example, snitching. In the heyday of prohibition and organized crime in this country, there was a code, even within the organized-crime community, that you didn't snitch on one another. That made it very difficult for law enforcement and, as a result, law enforcement was not based on paying informers; for the most part, it was based on gathering evidence. So while that made it difficult for law enforcement in terms of prohibition, it meant there was a certain code within the community which was adhered to and which kept a certain semblance of respect, a certain semblance of order, if you will. When you have thrown that away—when everyone is a potential informer on everyone else— you destroy whatever minimal social cohesion there is in a community. And if you look at the poorer areas of most of our cities now, there are so many informers and undercover drug agents wandering about, and so many young people being overcharged and then threatened with huge prison sentences unless they give up the names of every friend and relative in sight for prosecution, that this has a wearing effect on the community. If you were to take prison as an example of a society run that way, you get results like the Santa Fe, New Mexico, prison, for example, which had the worst riot of this century in terms of violence and mayhem: people killed with blow torches and beheaded and what have you, mostly inmate-on-inmate violence.

The Humanist: When was this?

Miller: This was in the mid-1980s. Before the riots, when the warden took people around the prison and saw four or five inmates standing together talking, he would say to the visitors, "I own at least three of them." It was a prison run entirely by snitches, and, of course, it creates a *Stasi*-like society so that, when the lid blows, it's very hard to keep the violence in check. In effect, we have created exactly that kind of society in the inner city through our law-enforcement techniques.

The Humanist: How widespread is police brutality in the United States? Has the NCIA done any studies on that?

Miller: Well, certainly in terms of open brutality it's much less than what it used to be. But I think you see more and more the kind of thing that happened in Tucson, Arizona, not so long ago, where you had three fellows pressured to confess to a crime they knew absolutely nothing about, and finally actually confessing and giving details of the crime scene and so on. That is routine these days. *Nightline* did a marvelous program on it, and the one very telling clip that was used showed the FBI Academy teaching police officers this sort of technique: how to lie, how to mislead, how to put up pictures of a crime scene so that a person can pick up the details and be able to confess to being somewhere he never was. This kind of practice is now routine; we see it all the time. It's a system that can no longer be trusted.

The Humanist: But can the people who operate this system actually be that cynical?

Miller: I think a lot of them sincerely believe that the person is guilty *before* they manufacture the evidence. But I think it's more than that. I have no trust at all in prosecutors. I'm speaking very personally, but I think very often (to quote something I heard Jerry Spence say a couple years back) that for anyone to stay in that business these days they've got to be a little bit mentally unbalanced. I see a kind of zeal and a level of dishonesty on the part of prosecutors that is just appalling. It's something very insidious that's going on in the nation. I don't know what one can do about it. One proposal I've made is that no prosecutor be allowed to run for office—that they be appointed or, if they're elected, that they never be allowed to run again for any other office. Because it's become a media show, particularly in the federal courts, where prosecutors will stand on the courthouse steps and rant and rave and carry on and tell gross untruths. They're virtually unaccountable, and the media simply run with it because these days the criminal-justice system is a system run on sound-bites and throw-away lines. They're not interested in research, they're not interested in what works, they're not interested in anything that would lower crime—much less in anything decent or humane that's going to advance society. It's just a terribly corrupt system.

The Humanist: When you were on C-SPAN, Hubert Williams,

president of the Police Foundation, pointed out that, over the last decade, the prison population in the United States has *doubled*. By the end of the 1990s, do you think it will actually have doubled again? And if so, what will that tell us?

Miller: Well, the National Council on Crime and Delinquency has done an analysis that hasn't been published yet, but will be shortly, which carries to their final conclusions the recommendations of both the Clinton administration and the Republican leadership on crime control: such things as mandatory sentences with no parole; more prosecution of drug crimes; increased use of the death penalty; and so on. And the council predicts that, if we follow these recommendations, we will have within a very few years—certainly before the turn of the century—*7.5 million* people in prison. That's 7.5 million people in prison if we in fact put these soundbite-type recommendations that get such great applause into practice. Now, if current trends were to continue—and there's no reason to believe they won't—of that 7.5 million people, 4 million or more will be black. Well, there are only about 5.5 million black men between the ages of 18 and 39 in the nation. We're reaching a point where most age-eligible black men will either be in prison or on probation or parole—mostly in prison and camps.

We did a study here in the District of Columbia in 1992, and we found that, on any given day, 42 percent of all the 18- to 35-year-old black men living in D.C. were either in jail, in prison, on probation or parole, out on bond, or being sought on warrants. When we replicated the study in Baltimore, the figure was 56 percent. It doesn't take any great stretch of the imagination to see that we will have the majority of young black men imprisoned by the turn of the century, and the inner cities will be made up primarily of single women and children. That's where we're headed. And this is because we've tried to treat a wide array of complex social problems with the criminal-justice system. We've replaced the social safety net with the dragnet, if you will—and that would never be proposed, much less tolerated, much less advocated, were we talking about white people.

The Humanist: So what you're saying, then, is that race is the big, ugly secret that lies at the heart of U.S. crime policy.

Miller: Exactly. That's what it's all about, because statistically that's who we're locking up.

The Humanist: Let's talk about some of the crime stories that have been prominently featured in the media lately. I mean, you have the tourist murders in Florida which have been hyped to the hilt, and also the verdict just handed down in the Reginald Denny beating trial. . . .

Miller: Well, the two of them are very interesting. The murders in Florida, for example, were a story that all the major networks ran with. It was featured on all of the evening news magazines, like *Day One* and *20/20*, and they all had local juvenile judges who were yelling and screaming about not being able to be tough enough on juveniles: "We're being too permissive; the juvenile justice system has to be scrapped." Not a single one of those programs, nor the nightly news shows, appeared to have done their homework. Had they done so, they would have found that Florida is probably the most punitive state in the nation with reference to juveniles. Last year, Florida ran 16,000 kids through its adult jails. It waived 6,000 kids from juvenile court into adult court; it direct-filed on another 4,000 to 5,000 juveniles in adult court. Now compare that with Massachusetts, the state in which I set up the system and in which we *closed* all the state reform schools (and, incidentally, under a Republican governor). In 1992, Massachusetts couldn't have tried more than two dozen kids in its adult courts. And Massachusetts is no more unsafe than Florida. Massachusetts actually is in pretty good shape compared to demographically similar states. But Florida was presented as an example of a permissive system when, in fact, the truth is much different.

For example, I've been a monitor for the federal courts on jail overcrowding in northern Florida, in the Jacksonville-Duval County area, which has around 700,000 people. And Jacksonville-Duval County, on any one day, had 10 percent of all the black kids in adult jails *in the nation* locked in its local jail. And it will be closer to 20 percent soon, because the authorities are shooting to put 300 to 500 kids in that adult jail. It would have been front-page news if I'd had *three* kids in an adult jail in Massachusetts.

So the media don't bother to do their homework, and I think the reason they don't is, once again, because in Florida and elsewhere we are talking primarily about young black men. In actual, statistical terms, the crime rate in Florida was down last year—particularly the rate of violent crime against tourists. But you wouldn't know that. And the idea of focusing on tourist murders was an oddity, because there's something over 40 million tourists in Florida every year. It would be like focusing on men who were six feet tall and had blue eyes and determining how many of them were attacked last year; the statistic has virtually no meaning. I think the implied message, of course, was that they were white tourists attacked by young blacks; we're not about to treat that the same way as we would white-on-white crime. Incidentally, we do an awful lot of work with young black kids who've committed violent crimes. There's just very little understanding of what they're all about; they're portrayed by the media in these horrendous, stereotypical terms.

The Humanist: Certainly one of the biggest obstacles to correcting those stereotypes is the political uses of crime policy. You have Bush running against Willie Horton in 1988, and also Clinton in 1992 going to Arkansas to preside over Ricky Ray Rector's execution.

Miller: That's right. When it comes to crime policy, there's not a dime's worth of difference between them.

The Humanist: But what about the new federal crime bill that's going through Congress now with the Clinton administration's support?

Miller: There's not much difference to it from previous bills. It's basically Joe Biden's bill, and Biden is horrendous on these issues. And Clinton's White House staff is infiltrated with a lot of Biden appointees, so I don't see much coming of it. If anything, the criminal-justice system needs to be *unwound;* it doesn't need to be intensified. We're running somewhere between 12 million and 14 million people a year through local jails—however, 80 percent of them are for misdemeanors. These people are getting criminal records; we now have 46 million criminal records in this country. In Jacksonville-Duval County, of a population of some 720,000 people, there were 330,000 criminal records. We are criminalizing a large proportion of the nation, and among minorities we are criminalizing the majority. Even conservative researchers like Al Blumstein at Carnegie Mellon have concluded that the average black man in this country can expect to be arrested and charged for a crime sometime during his life. The majority—over 50 percent—will be charged with a felony. It won't go anywhere, there won't be much to it, but they'll be arrested and charged with it. And 90 percent can expect to be arrested at least once for a misdemeanor. *Ninety percent,* at least once in their lifetime. This estimate comes from a very conservative socio-econometrist who was an advisor to the Reagan-Bush administration.

Now, I have no quarrel at all with those who want to get violent criminals off the street—no quarrel at all. But in the process, we're criminalizing a large portion of nonviolent people and we're creating a lot more violence. I mean, you do not just willy-nilly arrest a father in front of a son, or break into someone's house after some kind of minor drug dealing and throw everyone onto the floor in front of screaming children and upset mothers, and drag people off the way we are now doing routinely in our inner cities, without having it come back at you. You create anger. It's a sad commentary, but I think eminently true, that the most honest commentators on this situation are the rap groups. What they have to say is awful to hear, but it's the clearest explication of what impact this is having. And you don't hear it from the black leadership, which is so often separated now from what's happening in the community. Here in Washington, they're mostly middle-class, they live in the northwest part of the city away from all the squalor and crime, and they're indistinguishable from the white leadership on this issue.

The Humanist: Do you agree at all with what I think is a recurrent conservative notion: that there's been a vast moral breakdown throughout our society, and that this is the source of our problems with crime?

Miller: No, I don't. I think, as far as crime is concerned, that what we've seen is some class-crossing, if you will, that we didn't see before. Crime has left the restricted areas it used to be in and has begun to affect middle-class people. I don't see the situation the way it's being proposed now by Daniel Patrick Moynihan and others. It's a winning formula politically; it sounds great. But it's an elitist notion that betrays little understanding of what's going on in the community—particularly in the minority community.

One thing we see in dealing with average offenders—the kind of person that would be stereotyped as a serious, violent, savage-like street offender (and we see a lot of these young people here)—is that no one has ever spent any time with them finding out where they came from, what their life has been like, what's happened to them, why they would do what they did. Those are the kinds of things which we not only do *not* want to know but from which we run in fear—because if we were to hear them, we'd all feel a little bit guilty. We'd all have to do something, we'd have to get involved, and we don't want that. It's much easier to start talking about people in genetic terms or as "born criminals" or as somehow or other racially flawed.

You may recall that last year the University of Maryland had scheduled a conference on the "genetics of crime" in which James

Q. Wilson was to be the lead-off speaker. And it put out a bro-chure really hinting—more than hinting—that crime was genet-ically based (and, by implication, racially based). After it came to light (a lot of it having to do with NCIA's interest in it), there was upset within the black community, and the National Institute of Mental Health, which was going to fund the conference, pulled back from its funding—although I hear it's going to re-fund it again. Clearly, these are ominous turns, and they reflect the way criminological research is headed. It's become very much management-oriented; it's the kind of research that emanated from the Pentagon for many years. It's mainly head counts—there's very little anthropological methodology, there's very little feel for what people are all about, and there's very little narrative to it. It's the kind of thing that eminent psychologists like Jerome Brunner have been writing about—how we've lost the sense of narrative and, therefore, the human dimensions of much of this. And, of course, when you're talking about crime and criminals, it's very, very easy to fall into demonization and stereotyping. Not only will people accept it, you can build a political career around it.

The Humanist: It's true, too, that the way we define crime serves certain political and economic and social interests at the expense of many others.

Miller: It surely does.

The Humanist: I've been seeing articles lately about corruption and fraud at the Resolution Trust Corporation, the organization that's supposed to be cleaning up the savings and loan debacle. And those guys pulled off the biggest bank job in history; they ripped off far more money than every criminal in the inner city combined!

Miller: That's true. But there's a great mythology even about the amount of violent crime, you know; it's overhyped and overstated. Now I don't want to minimize the fact that we have too many murders and too many muggings; but if you look at the rates of violent crime over the past two decades, there has not been that much change. There was a sea change, and a very large rise in crime, after World War II—maybe 10 or 15 years after, about 1960 or so, as that baby boom started to get into the crime-prone ages from the mid-teens up to the mid-twenties. Crime had been falling from about 1934 or 1935 pretty much all the way through 1960—there'd been a couple of slight blips but, for the most part, it had been going down, including violent crime. And then, of course, it grew exponentially between 1960 and 1972, much of it attributable to the baby boom. But from 1972 on, there has not been that much dramatic change. It went down from 1972 or 1973 until about 1980, and in 1981 it went way up again. Then it went down until the drug war began, and then it went way up again. But as a whole, the violent-crime rate has been vastly overhyped.

The Humanist: You said that when the drug war started the crime rate went up. . . .

Miller: Well, the violence rate in particular, and I think it was largely attributable to our law-enforcement strategies for dealing with drugs. I think it was a direct result of criminalizing a lot of activities and then throwing away the rule book on how you deal with them. Certainly we threw away the Constitution when it came to the drug war.

The Humanist: What kind of alternatives do you think are available for making the criminal-justice system more just?

Miller: It's such a large industry now, I don't know. I think it's a matter of beginning to unwind it. We don't need *more* police, we need *less* police, and the police we have on the street should be focused on specific kinds of violent crime. But if they're going to have more police, and if they want to get back to the bucolic days of the 1930s, then the quality of policing will have to change. Back then, the police were a part of the community. They knew the neighborhood stores and most of the people and families in the community, and, very frankly, they ignored a great deal of illegal behavior. They handled things informally: they met with parents and their kids, they did all those things. An Irish cop in an Irish borough in New York City or in Boston certainly didn't deal with crime the way it's dealt with today, and the fact is he didn't deal with it in a tougher manner, he dealt with it in a more *humane* manner.

But now that we're dealing primarily with minority groups, particularly people of color, there's less and less of that happening— Los Angeles being the prime example of a militaristic, formal police model that has created its own gangs. I mean, the gangs in Los Angeles are a creation of the criminal-justice system. You aren't a gang leader unless you've been to one of the state prisons or the juvenile halls. Only the criminal-justice system could create groups like Noistra Familia and the Mexican Mafia and the White Aryan Brotherhood and the Crips and the Bloods and the Symbionese Liberation Army and all these crazy kinds of counterreactions, if you will, to law-enforcement intrusion into the lives of average folks. And I don't see that changing.

Former New York City Police Commissioner Lee Brown was accused of ignoring crime when he dissolved the tactical narcotics squad and had a lot less hassling of people in the neighborhoods. I think he was going in precisely the right direction and, in fact, the statistics available in New York City indicate that he was. Arrests went down, but so did violent crime, including homicide. And homicide is a reported crime—it wouldn't go down because people weren't reporting it. But, sadly, now that he's in the Clinton administration, he's backtracking on that. I noticed in his presentation on drug policy that he talked about the need to arrest minor drug offenders. Well, if they head back in that direction, they're going to be in big trouble again. There's a need to unwind; there's a need to find options—a lot of options—for the lesser offenders who are now going to jail and prison. We need to put an end to much of the jailing we do. As I say, 80 percent of the people brought into our jails are there for misdemeanors and lesser felonies.

The Humanist: Mainly for minor drug offenses? Drug possession?

Miller: An awful lot for what's called public-order offenses: drunkenness, trespassing, minor shoplifting. In our society, where the classes have become increasingly separated, where the rich get richer and the poor get poorer, the jails are now what sociologist John Irwin calls places of "rabble management." We have taken away funding from other programs that should be dealing with this, and many of the programs that still remain have been professionalized to the point where the people who run them refuse to deal with anyone who causes problems. And so they are dumped on the police and they end up in jail. Mental-health clinics, for example, ought to be open around the clock, not from nine to five, and they ought to be dealing with the more intractable and difficult street people, not with the articulate and verbal psychotherapy candidates. But none of this is happening, of course. The result is that a lot of folks have fallen into the criminal-justice system. And the criminal-justice system, if there's anything we do know about it, usually makes matters worse. The best service you can do for anyone who finds themselves caught up in the criminal-justice system is to get them out of it as quickly as possible. There are some very dangerous and violent people who must be placed in it for public-safety reasons, but the majority of people in it should be out of it and under other sorts of supervision or receiving other sorts of services. But I don't think that will happen. I think we will increasingly rely upon the criminal-justice system as a means of managing the underclass.

The Humanist: But how long can that possibly go on?

Miller: It will go on until it changes the very nature of our society. And if we reach a point where we have five million to seven million people in our prisons and jails, we will be a very different society from anything we've ever been in our history. As Nils Christie comments, we'll be a gulag society. And I think that's precisely what will happen. I'm not suggesting that the prisons will become concentration camps. I think they'll be much more benign—although I don't think we should discount the possibility of some of them moving in that direction, especially when you look at the so-called maxi-maxi prisons which have been recently developed across the country.

The Humanist: What are they?

Miller: They are the places being built to house those people who supposedly pose a "management problem" within the prison system—not necessarily people who have committed horrendous crimes but people who sass back or don't go where they're told, etc., etc. And based upon the federal model, which the national human-rights organizations see as a violation of basic human rights—the Marion Prison in Illinois, Pelican Bay in California, the one up in Baltimore; a number of states are doing this—they're horrendous. A very eminent professor friend of mine, one of the premiere sociologists in this country, visited the one in Baltimore and told me that, were this prison discovered after World War II, the people running it would be up for war crimes. People are kept in isolation or with white light on them all the time; they're subjected to sensory deprivation of the worst sort.

The Humanist: But when you talk to people or give lectures or appear on call-in shows or whatever, do you get a sense that people know what the prison system in this country actually is like?

Miller: No, but I don't think they really care, either. And that's because we're talking about black men; I don't know how else to say it. If you look at the average maxi-maxi prison, it will be certainly 60 to 80 percent black or more. If you look at the average state reform school now, it's the same—and I know the juvenile system very, very well. In Maryland, they're running 80 to 90 percent black, and no way is the population of Maryland 80 to 90 percent black, and no way are 80 to 90 percent of the kids in these places put there for anything like violent crime. And what I hear from my liberal friends—"Well, we may have lost a generation"—confirms to me that, in fact, they've judged young black males to be expendable. So when they start talking about dealing with root causes in terms of early childhood care, prenatal care, and so on, that's very nice; but I think it is also a way to avoid dealing with the reality that we already are trashing a generation and feel quite comfortable doing it.

The Humanist: If you could address the root causes, what would they be?

Miller: I think I'd be very traditional, very conservative in answering that question. I think it has to do with the family. When you look into the individual cases of kids, particularly those who've been involved in violent crime and who participated personally in the violence . . . because you have to realize that for the large proportion of so-called violent crimes, no one did anything physically violent. In 90 percent of violent crimes, no one even required medical attention; less than 5 percent require any kind of even minimal hospital care—

The Humanist: Then how does it get categorized as "violent" crime?

Miller: Someone makes a threat of violence. But if you look at someone who has actually shot or stabbed someone, who personally engages and is able to engage in some horrific crime of violence, then the story is the same across the board—white, black, brown, whatever. They are usually folks who come from horrendous backgrounds; they've been subjected to all sorts of violence in their own lives; they hold life at very little value, as their own lives have been held. And this is not to excuse them but to suggest that we need to understand where this comes from and begin to deal with those kinds of problems. The amount of family abuse, sexual abuse, personal abuse, physical abuse within the family among these folks is just horrendous. The NCIA has done death-penalty mitigative studies on a couple hundred of them—it's just routine in these kinds of cases—and the personal violence that these people have themselves suffered is appalling.

The Humanist: I think that's undeniably true, and it certainly seems simple enough to understand. So why do you think our society has such an enormous problem grasping it?

Miller: Because we're dealing with black men. We don't want to know what goes on. We don't want to know about their life situation—particularly poor blacks. And incidentally, upper-class blacks don't want to know it any more than whites. Very often, they run from it as fast as the white power structure does.

The Humanist: Well, but that sounds all the more like the real issue is class, not race.

Miller: It is class, but ultimately in terms of the white community I think it's race. I don't think you would see this if it were primarily poor whites; I don't think you'd see this kind of viciousness if it were mostly tow-headed, poor Appalachian kids. It's quite different. Believe it or not, there are a large number of sociologists who still very strongly maintain that there is no racial bias in the criminal-justice system—you know, that everybody's dealt with equally and fairly. And for anyone to say that tells me the level of discourse in this country. These guys have never been in a normal courthouse, sat at a hearing, talked to an offender, or spent time with a jail inmate or his family. But there are many studies now— I outline them in my book—that clearly show a sort of cumulative process of discrimination that builds at every level of the criminal-justice system: through arrests, through charging, through jailing, and so on. It affects the decision to give bond, whether you're released on recognizance, whether you have to show up for your sentencing in prison dungarees or your own suit, the kind of sentence you get, whether or not you get drug treatment, whether you're going to be tried as a juvenile or as an adult—all of this is racially biased, all of it is to some extent racially determined.

Unfortunately, it's politically incorrect to talk about race these days. No one wants to hear about it until it's forced on them through a riot or something. The verdict in the Reginald Denny beating trial, which you mentioned earlier, provides the best example of what's going on underneath the surface. The reaction in the black community was that it was a pretty good verdict, and I would tend to agree with that, because I think those fellows were overcharged. Clearly, they should've been charged with aggravated assault or something like that—

The Humanist: But when you say "overcharged," do you mean they were too punitively charged or that every possible charge was piled on top of them?

Miller: They were charged with these crimes that would carry life sentences. The district attorney's office just got so vicious on this that even the jury couldn't buy it. And I don't believe the jury was frightened, I think the prosecutors probably couldn't sustain such charges. I think they would have been better off, if they were looking for a harsher sentence, to come in with a different charge around aggravated assault; they probably would have gotten them more years than they did with all the crazy charges around mayhem.

But the reaction to the verdict is what I think is more telling.

To a large percentage of the white community, the verdict was seen as *favoring* blacks, as letting these guys off too lightly. I don't think it's a correct perception, but it was the majority reaction, and I think that kind of dictates where we're headed. It's the same kind of thing as when the jury in the Simi Valley trial could look at those beatings by the police and somehow say that this seemed okay, it was just part of police procedure. It's bizarre to me that that could have happened.

So I see things as getting much more racially polarized, and I think the laws will reflect that. I don't think we'll go in the direction of being more humane. And I certainly don't think it matters that Los Angeles stayed calm, that no one got all worked up after the verdict—that's beside the point. We want our pound of flesh. We don't care what happens. We want to prove a point with blacks, and we're going to do it with the criminal-justice system.

THE ECONOMICS OF CRIME[4]

Americans are scared. The fear of crime permeates their lives. They worry about being mugged or raped in a parking lot or while walking home from work. They're afraid of being robbed at a highway rest stop or having their children kidnapped at a suburban mall. They put bars on their windows, alarms in their cars, and cans of tear gas in their pockets. And they should be frightened. All told, some 14 million serious crimes were re ported to the police last year, a number that surely understates the actual magnitude of America's No. 1 problem.

But the daily reality of muggings and murders that make the headlines and TV news shows is hurting the public in a far different, yet no less destructive, way. Crime in America is exacting an enormous economic toll on the nation—far bigger than anyone realizes.

New estimates by *Business Week* show that crime costs Americans a stunning $425 billion each year. That figure comes from a detailed analysis of all of the direct and indirect costs of both property and violent crimes, from emergency-room care for a

---

4 Article by Michael J. Mandel and Paul Magnusson from *BusinessWeek* D. 13, '93. Copyright © 1993 by BusinessWeek. Reprinted by permission.

mugging victim to the price of a new alarm system for a home to the income lost to the family of a murdered cab driver.

Human misery aside, from a purely dollars-and-sense perspective, the U.S. isn't devoting enough resources to the fight against crime—and is frittering away many of the resources it is using. The U.S. spends some $90 billion a year on the entire criminal-justice system. That includes $35 billion for police protection, less than the country is spending on toiletries each year. Indeed, anticrime policy over the years has been a series of quick, cheap fixes: new prisons are being built, but the number of police has barely kept pace with the growing population. Meanwhile, economic and social programs that could quickly bring down crime have been largely ignored.

Even the spate of crime-fighting legislation going through Congress falls far short of what is needed. The Brady bill, just signed into law, simply requires a five-day waiting period for the purchase of handguns. And the highly acclaimed anticrime bill recently passed by the Senate would add a meager $4.5 billion a year to total criminal-justice spending.

TV Violence. Why is the nation underspending on crime-fighting? The public may well believe that there's little more money can do short of putting the Army on every street corner. Some have blamed crime and violence on the decline of "family values" or the loss of inner-city manufacturing jobs, neither of which can be solved by government action. Most recently, excessive violence on tv has been fingered as a key culprit by Attorney General Janet Reno and Surgeon-General M. Joycelyn Elders.

Economists, on the other hand, view crime as a choice that can be affected by changes in punishments and rewards. Recent research by economists shows that higher levels of anticrime spending, if well-directed, can make a big dent in crime. Crime can be reduced by increasing what economists call the "expected punishment"—the average prison time served for a crime, adjusted for the chances of being caught and convicted. Today, the expected punishment for committing a serious crime is only about 11 days—half what it was in the 1950s. At the same time, job prospects for young adults and teenagers have soured, lowering the economic rewards for staying straight. "Criminals are sensitive to incentives," says Morgan O. Reynolds, a Texas a&m University economist who studies the economics of crime. Adds Ann Witte, a Wellesley economist: "The carrot can work, and the stick can work."

What's needed is a cost-effective way of raising the punishment that potential criminals can expect, argue these economists.
That means the U.S. needs to devote many more resources to
every aspect of law enforcement, not just prisons. That means
more police on the streets, tougher sentences for young criminals,
and closer monitoring of criminals on probation.

At the same time, it's crucial that the U.S. boost spending for
job training and other programs in order to give teenagers and
young adults better alternatives to crime. Typically, these programs are cheaper than the $20,000- to $30,000-a-year cost of
imprisonment. "We will never be able to afford enough prisons if
that's our only approach to the criminal-justice problem," says
Stephen Goldsmith, the Republican mayor of Indianapolis and a
district attorney for 12 years. "You have to give people some hope
for jobs and housing."

Such sentiments are far more common today than they were
just a few years ago. In the 1980s, politicians were quick to call for
longer, harsher sentences for all types of crimes. And one of the
most damaging labels for a local politician in those years was "soft
on crime." Yet for all the harsh rhetoric, few additional resources
were devoted to fighting crime on the streets. Spending on prisons and the judicial system soared in the 1980s, but the number
of police per 10,000 people barely rose. Indeed, in the second
half of the decade, the total number of state and local police
increased by only 16 percent, while the number of violent crimes
jumped by 37 percent.

Now, fiscally strapped local officials find themselves begging
for federal help and admitting defeat. District of Columbia May-
or Sharon Pratt Kelly unsuccessfully sought to deploy National
Guard troops on the capital's streets, saying: "We're dealing with a
war, yet people don't seem to want to win this war." After three
hundred stores were robbed and 52 people killed during holdups
this year, Kelly's police chief recently suggested that a good way to
cut crime was to close stores earlier.

The analogy to war is a good one. By *Business Week's* calcula-
tion, the real cost of violent and property crime—when properly
toted up—far exceeds the $300 billion defense budget. Spend-
ing by businesses and consumers on private security alone—
including alarms, guards, and locks—comes to some $65 billion,
according to William Cunningham, president of Hallcrest Systems Inc., a McLean (Va.) security-industry consulting firm.
"People are more fearful, and they're taking a greater stake in

their own protection." This has turned into a bonanza for companies such as Winner International Corp. in Sharon, Pa., which engineers and markets The Club, a steering-wheel lock to discourage auto theft. From 1990 to 1992, Club sales grew from $22 million to $107.3 million.

But Winner's bonanza is just another burden for business and consumers. "I call this the 'security tax' that business now has to pay because government hasn't been able to make us feel safe at home, work, or play," says Frank J. Portillo Jr., chief executive of Brown's Chicken & Pasta Inc., a one-hundred-store fast-food chain based in Oak Brook, Ill. He had to install security cameras and hire guards for some of his stores in rougher neighborhoods after seven employees were massacred on January 8 at a Brown's Chicken outlet in Palatine, Ill.

The security tax hits urban areas particularly hard. According to *Business Week*'s analysis of FBI crime statistics, most large cities have violent crime rates from two to seven times higher than their suburbs. As a result, many businesses and residents of crime-prone areas move to safer surroundings. That can quickly become a self-perpetuating cycle, since as jobs move out, the area becomes even more hopeless for the people who remain. *Business Week* estimates that annual damage to large urban economies from high crime rates is about $50 billion.

Miami Vise. Because of Miami's dependence on tourism, it is probably the urban area facing the clearest threat from crime. The city "has two problems," says Joseph P. Lacher, president of Miami-based Southern Bell-Florida and chairman of the Greater Miami Chamber of Commerce. "We have a serious crime problem to deal with and an even worse perception of crime." Dade County, where Miami is located, has one of the highest crime rates in the country. "People are scared to come to Florida," says Roberto Willimann, owner of Specialized Travel Systems, a Miami travel agency that caters to Germans. His business fell to about half of last year's after the September 8 murder of a German tourist.

But crime's most devastating impact is measured in more than lost jobs and added security costs. The victim of a mugging or a rape carries the physical and emotional scars for years. Moreover, the damage to friends, family, and society from every murder is enormous.

Economists are able to measure the economic value of such intangible damages of violent crime using techniques originally developed for the cost-benefit analysis of safety regulations. According to newly published estimates by Ted R. Miller, a health-and-safety economist at National Public Services Research Institute in Landover, Md., and two colleagues, the value of a human life cut short by murder is about $2.4 million. They estimate the economic damage of a rape to average about $60,000, while the typical robbery or assault costs more than $20,000. With more than 20,000 murders committed each year plus two million other crimes of violence, the so-called intangible damages come to a mind-numbing $170 billion, says Miller and his co-authors.

If America really wants to bring down violent crime, there's simply no way of dealing cheaply with a problem of this magnitude. "If you are going to have an effect, you have to spend a lot of money," says Wellesley economist Witte.

But in a time of belt-tightening, it's essential to make every dollar as effective as possible. The ultimate goal is to reduce the incentives for criminal behavior. "We need the positives from participating in the legitimate economy to go up and the negatives from participating in the criminal economy to go up," says Goldsmith. "We've got the mix exactly backward."

Diminishing Returns. Spending on corrections has quadrupled over the past decade, rising far faster than spending on police or the courts. In part, that has been because of court-ordered upgrades of existing prisons, but actual incarcerations in state and federal prisons have tripled since 1980. And some economists, like Texas A&M's Reynolds, believe that this prison boom has helped boost expected punishment a bit, keeping the crime problem from getting even worse than it already is.

But now the law of diminishing returns is setting in. Building and staffing prisons is extremely expensive, especially as sentences get longer and older inmates require increased medical care. Imprisoning a 25-year-old for life costs a total of $600,000 to $1,000,000. So putting someone in prison for life puts a huge financial burden on the next generation—just as a big budget deficit does.

For that reason, much of the additional spending on law enforcement should go toward beefing up police forces rather than building new prisons. Indeed, evidence from economic studies shows that putting more police on the front lines has more of a deterrent effect than longer prison sentences. Explains Judge Richard Fitzgerald of Jefferson District Family Court in Louisville: "Most cops I know think that what really deters is the certainty of apprehension, not the sanction that would be imposed."

Even so, any concerted attempt to raise expected punishment will necessarily mean spending more on prisons. Every year, more than 60,000 violent criminals receive probation, largely because of overcrowding, according to Michael Block, a University of Arizona economist who was a member of the U.S. Sentencing Commission. That means one of the cheapest solutions to the crime problem, he says, is to "punish those people who are already captured."

Few Worries. But the largest holes are in the juvenile-justice system. Violent-crime rates among young people have been rising far faster than among adults. "We are seeing juveniles committing more of the violent crimes at a younger age and with more destructive force and impact," says Judge Fitzgerald.

Part of the problem is that expected punishment for juveniles is very low. Young people often get little punishment for the first three or four felonies. "Juveniles have been getting the message that they can get away with anything," says Marvin Wolfgang, a criminologist at the University of Pennsylvania. Adds Mark A. Kleiman, an expert in the economics of crime at Harvard University: "It trains people to be criminals."

In addition, teenagers have little worry that crimes committed as juveniles will hurt them as adults. In most states, juvenile criminal records are permanently sealed. So a cost-effective way of identifying multiple offenders would be to unseal juvenile criminal records at the first adult felony conviction.

America's solution for dealing with illegal drug use has cost it dearly, too. In the 1980s, draconian sentencing laws were used to combat the drug problem, putting tens of thousands of people—and not necessarily the most violent ones—in prison. Currently, 60 percent of inmates in federal prisons and 20 percent of inmates in state prisons are there on drug charges. That helped drive up spending on prisons without doing much to deter violent crime.

One alternative strategy to keep down drug use and related crime without filling up scarce prison cells is to monitor more closely the nearly three million convicts on probation. Kleiman argues that regular drug-testing of criminals on probation could dramatically reduce drug use, at a cost of perhaps $5 billion annually. That can be combined with increased funding for drug-rehab programs like the one at DC General Hospital in Washington, which treats nine hundred people each year at a cost of about $1,800 per person. "Most people who are heavy users can and will quit if they are under heavy pressure," says Kleiman, "and you'll reduce the criminal activities of the people you're testing."

But by itself, increased enforcement will not be enough to stem the tide of violence. "Short term, we need more cops and more aggressiveness in enforcement and prosecution," says Louisville Mayor Jerry Abramson, chairman of the U.S. Conference of Mayors. "But when a police officer gets involved, that's too late. The focus has to be not just on catching criminals but on preventing criminals."

Moreover, giving young people alternatives to crime can multiply the effectiveness of the existing criminal-justice system. For every person not committing crimes, police can concentrate more resources on hard-core criminals. For example, if job training and education programs lowered the crime rate by 25 percent, that could mean an increase of as much as one-third in the expected punishment for lawbreakers.

Unlike many social programs, intensive training and education have already provided good evidence that they can reduce the crime rate. "Crime is a young man's game," says Witte. "Keep them busy and doing things that are not illegal, and they don't get in trouble."

For example, studies of the federal Job Corps, which is a residential program for basic education and hands-on vocational training, show a big drop in arrests for program participants. "There are few programs for young men that we can document as working well," says David Long, a senior research associate at Manpower Demonstration Research Corp., a nonprofit research organization in New York. "The Job Corps stands out as strikingly effective."

A New World. The key to the success of the Job Corps and similar private programs is providing kids with a whole new environment. That makes such programs expensive to run: a year in the Job Corps costs about $22,000. Adding enough slots in these programs to make a difference could cost billions. About 650,000 juveniles were arrested in 1992 for violent and property crimes. To provide programs for half of them would cost about $7 billion annually.

These programs are cheaper than the prisons they could replace, though. Average per-inmate cost for all juvenile facilities nationwide runs at about $30,000 annually. That's far more than the yearly cost of a slot in the Job Corps. In some cases, the difference can be even bigger. Take City Lights School in Washington, with one hundred inner-city adolescents, many of them violent juvenile offenders. According to Stephen E. Klingelhofer, development director at City Lights, the $53-a-day cost is a bargain compared with the $147 daily tab at Lorton Reformatory Youth Center in Lorton, Va. Treatment at City Lights can be as simple as setting a good example. "A lot of these kids have never seen anyone getting up in the morning and going to a job," says Klingelhofer. "A lot of them come here not knowing any other way to settle disputes than by violence."

More and more police departments are focusing on prevention as well. This new philosophy goes under the name of "community policing," which means reorganizing police departments to put more officers in the field and focusing on helping neighborhoods prevent crime rather than just reacting to emergencies. That approach may include having more police out walking beats, working with social service and community agencies, and generally getting to know the residents. "We want to improve the quality of life in the neighborhoods," says Jerry Galvin, police chief of Vallejo, Calif., which has used community policing for six years and seen violent crime drop by 33 percent.

If combined with organizational reforms, a shift to community policing need not mean a huge expenditure of new resources, advocates say. "Community policing has nothing to do with new officers or more money," says Galvin. "But you have to remake the department to make community policing work." In Vallejo, 80 percent of police officers are in the field vs. the national average of about 60 percent.

New Haven, Conn., has had the same experience. In early 1993, New Haven shifted to community policing rather than just having officers answer 911 calls. That required more police on the street. The solution: substitute civilian staff for cops who used to pump gas into police cruisers and hand out billy clubs and clip boards. It's cost-effective as well. An officer costs about twice as much as a clerical worker and is much more expensive to train.

Vicious Cycle. Part of what's scary about the latest wave of crime is not just the numbers but the brutality involved, especially the rampant use of firearms. From 1986 to 1991, robberies increased by 27 percent, but the use of a firearm during a robbery increased by 49 percent. And in a vicious cycle, crime is escalating the number of guns in private hands, as frightened Americans search for protection. At Colt Manufacturing Co. in Hartford, Conn., commercial handgun sales are running about 25 percent higher in 1993 than they were in 1992. "A whole gamut of industries are supplying the services that are being created by the crime statistics," says Colt Chairman R. C. Whitaker.

Can this spiral of violence be broken? Certainly a federal law making handguns illegal would sharply decrease the number of guns being sold and make their street price much higher, though, like prohibition in the 1920s or the war against drugs in the 1980s, it might be very expensive to enforce. But with 60 million handguns already in private hands, even an effective ban on guns might not be enough. One intriguing possibility is to return to an approach that has been tried successfully in the past—buying back handguns. In 1974, the City of Baltimore decided to offer $50 per gun. In three months, 13,792 guns were turned in. A similar program today could help get illegally owned guns off the street, especially if combined with national gun control.

Some groups are trying to stamp out juvenile crime before it starts by teaching kids that violence simply is not the only way to settle disputes. That approach can be cost-effective, experts say, if it is started early. For example, Howard University's Violence Prevention Project is trying to teach 40 troubled fourth, fifth, and sixth graders to cope with boredom, frustration, and anger without reaching for a weapon. "Is it working? It's too early to tell," admits Hope Hill, director of the program. "It appears to be, but it will take several years to know."

In the end, no one solution will work, and no cheap and easy cure is possible. But the tremendous cost of crime to Americans demands that we not give up. The country's great wealth can surely be harnessed in an effective way to provide the remedies that will allow people to walk the streets without fear again.

BIBLIOGRAPHY

Books and Pamphlets

An asterisk (*) preceding a reference indicates an excerpt from the work has been reprinted in this book.

Abadinsky, Howard. Organized crime. Nelson-Hall. '94.

Adler, Freda, et al. Criminal justice. McGraw-Hill. '94.

Aguirre, Adalberto & David V. Baker. Race, racism, and the death penalty in the United States. Vande Vere. '91.

Albanese, Jay S. & Robert D. Pursley. Crime in America: some existing and emerging issues. Prentice-Hall. '93.

Allen, Harry E. & Clifford E. Simonsen. Corrections in America. Macmillan. '92.

Ammons, David N., et al. The option of prison privitization. Carl Vincent Institute, U. S. Government. '92.

Bart, Pauline & Eileen Moran. Violence against women. Sage. '93.

Berns, Walter. For capital punishment. University Press of America. '91.

Bohm, Robert, ed. The death penalty in America. Anderson. '91.

Borak, Gregg, ed. Media, process, and the social construction of crime. Garland. '94.

Churchill, Ward, ed. The politics of imprisonment in the United States. Maisoneuve. '92.

Closter, Daniel S. Bad guys and good guys: moral polarization and crime. Greenwood. '92.

Croall, Hazel. White collar crime. Open University Press. '92.

Cummins, Eric. The rise and fall of California's radical prison movement. Stanford University Press. '94.

Currie, Elliott. Reckoning: drugs, the cities, and the American future. Hill & Wang. '93.

Davies, Malcolm. Punishing criminals. Greenwood. '93.

Davis, John H. The rise and fall of the Gambino crime family. Harper Collins. '93.

Dembo, Richard & Linda E. Williams, eds. Drugs and crime. University Press of America. '93.

Denno, Debora W. Biology and violence: from birth to adulthood. Cambridge University Press. '90.

Dicks, Shirley. Interviews with inmates, their families, and opponents of capital punishment. McFarland. '90.

Dubro, James. Dragons of crime inside the Asian underworld. Octopus. '92.

Finkelman, Paul. Race and criminal justice. Garland. '92.

Forer, Lois G. A rage to punish: the unintended consequences of mandatory sentencing. Norton. '94.

Friedman, Lawrence. Crime and punishment in American history. Basic Books. '93.

Gambetta, Diego. The Sicilian mafia. Harvard University Press. '93.

Hamm, Mark S. American skinheads: the criminology and control of hate crime. Praeger. '93.

———, ed. Hate crime: international perspectives on causes and control. Anderson. '94.

Harrell, Adele & George E. Peterson, eds. Drugs, crime, and social isolation. Urban Institute Press. '92.

Harris, Robert. Crime, criminal justice and the probation service. Routledge. '92.

Heiland, Hans-Gunther, et al, eds. Crime and control in comparative perspectives. De Gruyter. '91.

Herek, Gregory M. & Kevin T. Berrill, eds. Hate crimes. Sage. '92.

House, H. Wayne & John H. Yoder. The death penalty debate. Word. '93.

Inciardi, James A. The war on drugs, II. Mayfield. '92.

———, et al. Street kids, street drugs, street crime. Wadsworth. '93.

Irwin, John & James Austin. It's about time: America's imprisonment binge. Wadsworth. '94.

Kappeler, Victor E., et al. The mythology of crime and criminal justice. Waveland. '93.

Knox, George. An introduction to gangs. Vande Vere. '91.

Lab, Steven P. Crime prevention: approaches, practices, and evaluation. Anderson. '92.

Lavigne, Yves. Hell's Angels. Carol. '93.

Lea, John & Jock Young. What is to be done about law and order? Pluto. '93.

Levin, Jack & Jack McDevitt. Hate crimes: the rising tide of bigotry and bloodshed. Plenum. '93.

Locke, Trevor. New approaches to crime in the 1990s. Longman. '90.

Lotz, Roy. Crime and the American press. Praeger. '91.

Lynch, Michael J. & E. Britt Patterson. Race and criminal justice. Harrow & Heston. '91.

Mackenzie, Doris L. & Craig D. Uchida, eds. Drugs and crime. Sage. '94.

Mann, Coramae R. Unequal justice: a question of color. Indiana University Press. '93.

Martin, Robert P. The death penalty: God's will or man's folly. Simpson. '92.

Mathews, Roger. Rethinking criminology: the realist debate. Sage. '92.

Mathiessen, Thomas. Prison on trial. Sage. '91.

McMurran, Mary & Clive R. Hollin. Young offenders and alcohol-related crime. Wiley. '93.

Mieckowski, Thomas. Drugs, crime, and social policy. Allyn & Bacon. '92.

Monk, Richard C. Taking sides: clashing views on controversial issues in crime and criminology. Duskin. '93.

Morris, Norval & Michael Tonry. Between prison and probation: intermediate punishments in a rational sentencing system. Oxford University Press. '90.

Moyer, Imogene L., ed. The changing roles of women in the criminal justice system. Waveland. '92.

Nardo, Don. Death penalty. Lucent. '92.

National Issues Forum Staff. Criminal violence: what direction now for the war on crime? Kendall-Hunt. '92.

Neubauer, David W. America's courts and the criminal justice system. Brooks/Cole. '92.

Olamigoke, Olumide K. How to reduce crime rates in America. American Literary Press. '94.

Petrakis, Gregory J. The new face of organized crime. Kendall-Hunt. '92.

Potter, Gary W. Criminal organizations. Waveland. '94.

Prejean, Helen. Dead man walking: an eyewitness account of the death penalty in the United States. Vintage. '94.

Randall, Denise. Drugs and organized crime. Watts. '90.

Rideout, Wilbert & Ron Wikberg. Life sentences: rage and survival behind bars. Times Books. '92.

Roberts, Albert, ed. Critical issues in crime and punishment. Sage. '94.

Rodriguez, Luis J. Always running: la vida loca: gang days in L. A. Curbstone. '93.

Russell, Gregory D. The death penalty and racial bias. Greenwood. '94.

Rutherford, Andrew. Criminal justice and the pursuit of decency. Oxford University Press. '93.

Savelsberg, Joachim J. & Peter Bruhl. Constructing white-collar crime. University of Pennsylvania Press. '94.

Schmalleger, Frank. Criminal justice today. Prentice-Hall. '93.

Scott, Kody. Monster: the autobiography of a L. A. gang member. Atlantic Monthly Press. '93.

Selke, William L. Prisons in crisis. Indiana University Press. '93.

Sellers, Martin P. The history and politics of private prisons. Fairleigh Dickinson University Press. '93.

Senna, Joseph J. & Larry J. Siegel. Introduction to criminal justice. West. '92.

Skogan, Wesley G. Disorder and decline: crime and the spiral of decay in American neighborhoods. Free Press. '90.

Spelman, W. Criminal incapacitation. Plenum. '93.

Stenson, Kevin & David Cowell. The politics of crime and control. Sage. '92.

Surette, Ray. Media, crime, and criminal justice. Brooks/Cole. '92.

Territo, Leonard, et al. Crime and justice in America: a human perspective. West. '92.

Tidwell, Mike. In the shadow of the White House: drugs, death, and redemption on the streets of the nation's capital. Prima. '92.

Tipp, Stacey L. American prisons. Greenhaven. '91.

Tonry, Michael & James Q. Wilson, eds. Drugs and crime. University of Chicago Press. '90.

Tushnet, Mark V. The death penalty. Facts on File. '94.

Vaksberg, Arkadii. The Soviet mafia. St. Martin's Press. '91.

Von Hirsch, Andrew & Andrew Ashworth, eds. Principled sentencing. Northeastern University Press. '92.

Voss, Anthony A. Alternatives to prison. Sage. '90.

Walker, Samuel. Sense and nonsense about crime and drugs. Wadsworth. '94.

Walters, Glenn D. Drugs and crime in a lifestyle perspective. Sage. '94.

Wekesser, Carol, ed. The death penalty. Greenhaven. '91.

Westermann, Ted D. & James W. Burfeind. Crime and justice in two societies: Japan and the United States. Wadsworth. '91.

Wheeler, Stanton, et al. Sitting in judgment: the sentencing of white-collar criminals. Yale University Press. '92.

Wright, Martin. Justice for victims and offenders: a restorative approach to crime. Wiley. '93.

Wright, Richard A. In defense of prisons. Greenwood. '94.

Zimring, Franklin E. & Gordon Hawkins. The scale of imprisonment. University of Chicago Press. '91.

Additional Periodical Articles with Abstracts

For those who wish to read more widely on the subject of language and language policy, this section contains abstracts of additional articles that bear on the topic. Readers who require a comprehensive list of materials are advised to consult the *Reader's Guide to Periodical Literature* and other Wilson indexes.

Reefer madness Eric Schlosser, *Atlantic Monthly* v274 p 45–9+ Ag '94

More people may be imprisoned today for violating marijuana laws than at any other time in U.S. history. Marijuana laws were made much tougher in the 1980s. As a result, an estimated 35,000 to 45,000 people are now in federal, state, and local prisons primarily for marijuana offenses. Supporters who campaign for marijuana's legalization view it as a benign recreational drug, a form of herbal medicine, and a product with industrial applications, but opponents argue that marijuana promotes irresponsible sexual behavior, encourages disrespect for traditional values, and harms the user's mental, physical, and spiritual well-being. The article discusses the history of marijuana cultivation and use in the U.S., scientific evidence concerning the health effects of marijuana use, the criminalization and decriminalization of marijuana in the U.S., and the cases of various Americans who have been imprisoned for violating marijuana laws.:BRDG94063767

Shock: it works! Tim Hendricks, *The Conservationist* v47 p 44–7 S/O '92

Since it began in 1987, New York's Shock Incarceration Program has put select nonviolent criminals to work on community service projects, including projects for the Department of Environmental Conservation, in exchange for early parole. The voluntary program provides prisoners with discipline, education, exercise, and intensive alcohol and substance abuse rehabilitation. With the first 4,411 graduates, as of September 30, 1991, Shock has saved New York taxpayers an estimated $177 million in both operating and capital costs and given recreationists the benefit of public land improvements. Discussed are the location of Shock facilities, the interior and trail work performed by the Moriah Shock unit in the Adirondacks, and the education Shock participants receive.

What to do about crime James Q. Wilson, *Commentary* v98 p 25–34 S '94

America has not one crime problem but at least two. One is high, though currently declining, rates of property crime. The other is high levels of violence—particularly among young people and gang members—that is produced disproportionately by an alienated and self-destructive underclass. Most of this violent crime is committed by a small group of people who share a number of temperamental and sociological traits. One way to address this problem is "problem-oriented policing," in which police would engage in directed patrol aimed at reducing the opportunities for these high-risk people to do things that increase the chances of their victimizing others. Drug tests, gun inspections, and enforcement of truancy and curfew laws are examples of this approach. Another strategy is to change policy toward single mothers so as to alter the ways in which at-risk children experience their early years. Penal and juvenile justice policy are also discussed.:BRDG94062722

Biting the bullet. Vicki Kemper, *Common Cause Magazine* v18 p 16–22 Wint '92

Former District of Columbia police chief Isaac Fulwood, Jr., who recently traded in his badge to direct the city's new Youth Initiatives Office, is among the advocates of a long-term social and economic approach to crime prevention. The Reagan and Bush administrations adopted a traditional, short-term policy that emphasized more police, more arrests, more prisons, and stiffer sentences. President-elect Bill Clinton does not differ much in his approach. The U.S. now has the highest incarceration rate of any industrialized nation, while for the second year in a row the country set a new murder record. Experts argue that to break the cycle of violence, U.S. families, churches, and community organizations, as well as local, state, and federal governments, must act to protect children from the ravages caused by increasing poverty, domestic abuse, urban decay, job loss, and a popular culture that continues to glorify and glamorize violence.

No justice by the numbers. Peter E. Ball, *Commonweal* v120 p 14–17 O 8 '93

The Federal Sentencing Guidelines, which went into effect on November 1, 1987, are well-intentioned, but they only substitute one imperfect system for another. The guidelines were aimed at rectifying the perceived inequities in the sentences handed down by U.S. federal trial judges. At the time, the judges were given broad sentencing options, with the result that different judges, often within the same jurisdiction, were meting out grossly disparate sentences for very similar cases. In an attempt to make sentencing more uniform, the guidelines superimpose onto the broad statutory ranges of penalties a narrower range of penalties that a judge must impose in any given case. The guidelines, however, fail to resolve the uniformity problem because virtually every case and every defendant is different and thus uniformity is unattainable. The case of Jesus Lopez-Gil, a drug courier who was arrested almost 3 years ago but whose sentence has yet to be decided, is discussed.

The Hells Angels' devilish business. Andrew Evan Serwer, *Fortune* v126 p 118–22 N 30 '92

Many members of the Hells Angels and other outlaw biker clubs are involved in crime. Federal law enforcement agencies say that outlaw bikers, with over 300 clubs, 5,000 members, and at least 10,000 regular hangers-on, form one of the largest organized criminal networks in the United States. The agencies believe that these outlaw gangs earn up to $1 billion a year worldwide through drug dealing, prostitution, gunrunning, theft, extortion, and murder. The largest and most sophisticated club, the Hells Angels boast about 1,000 members in more than 70 chapters worldwide, a tight management structure, sophisticated communications systems, and paramilitary discipline. After being battered by a series of investigations in the 1980s, the Hells Angels and 3 other major bike gangs—the Outlaws, Bandidos, and Pagan's—are building their membership back up and have become more secretive.

U.S. suburbs are under siege. Alan Farnham, *Fortune* v126 p 42–4 D 28 '92

A new wave of crime is frightening suburban residents and shoppers and has businesses scrambling for ways to cope. According to a 1991 survey by the National Opinion Research Council, more than 42 percent of residents in suburbs of major cities were afraid to walk in their neighborhoods. FBI statistics show that violent crime—robberies, rapes, aggravated assaults, murder, and manslaughter—has increased more than 30 percent between 1985 and 1991. On a crime per capita basis, suburbia was more dangerous in the 1970s, but people do not find comfort in such statistics once they learn of a rape or mugging at a local mall. Fear is affecting business, cutting further into the profits of retailers, who must spend a rising share of their profits to protect—or at least reassure—customers. Discussed are the ways that the rise in suburban crime is altering society.

Girlz n the hood. Suzanne O'Malley, *Harper's Bazaar* p 238–43+ 0 '93

A firestorm of national publicity fell on San Antonio in April, when the local Planned Parenthood office reported that several girl gang members had sex with an HIV-positive gang member. The story has been unsubstantiated, but the prevalence of gangs in the city is obvious. An estimated 12,000 kids ages 10 to 16 in San Antonio belong to one of 250 gangs; about 2,000 of these are girls, and the number is growing. The gangs cross all socioeconomic lines and include whites, Hispanics, and African-Americans. According to Donna Willborn of the San Antonio Police Department's Juvenile Investigations Unit, 3 types of girls are involved with gang life: sisters and girlfriends of gang members; wanna-bes, who live like members but don't claim a specific gang; and full-fledged, actual members. Two young female gang members are profiled.

Americans in cages. Barbara Dority, *The Humanist* v53 p 36–7 N/D '93

America's prison system does not work. Incarceration is an abusive and violent act that does nothing to make the public safer, compensate crime victims, or prepare prisoners to reenter society. Money is being squandered on high walls, barbed wire, motion detectors, and massive guard staffs at a time when the country's wealth is needed for training, education, drug rehabilitation, economic development, environmental improvement, and jobs. The U.S. currently imprisons more than 1 million people and keeps another 4 million under "correctional control" (in jails and on probation or parole). Prison costs currently range up to $30,000 per inmate per year. Dangerous repeat offenders must be kept in top-security facilities, but work-release programs and monitored "honor houses" would be more effective, cheaper, and more productive for the majority of prisoners.

Blacks, Jews, liberals, and crime. Ed Koch, *National Review* v46 p 34+ My 16 '94

An article adapted from a speech given by former New York Mayor Ed Koch at the National Review Institute's Washington Summit in March: The problem of black crime must be addressed. According to the Justice Department, 45 percent of violent crimes are committed by black males, who make up only 6 percent of the population. Racism cannot be blamed for the problem of black crime. In fact, the claim that it can only exacerbates the problem. Because black leaders and organizations have failed to deal with the problems of crime, drugs, and illegitimacy in the black community, they have embraced black Muslim leader Louis Farrakhan, who tells blacks that their problems are not their fault, but are everybody else's fault, especially the fault of the Jews. Punishment, incarceration, and mandatory national service for youth could help solve this problem. Responses from Jack Kemp, Walter E. Williams, Peter N. Kirsanow, Jared Taylor, and William F. Buckley Jr. are provided.

Jailhouse blues. Wesley Smith, *National Review* v46 p 40–4 Je 13 '94

The federal judiciary is responsible for the explosion of lawsuits instigated by inmates of state prisons. Since 1966, when prisoners filed a total of 218 suits to remedy arguably inhumane treatment, the federal judiciary has opened the floodgates. Prisoners filed 53,713 lawsuits in federal courts in 1993. Four-fifths of all state prison systems and roughly one-third of the five hundred largest local jails have been placed under federal-court supervision. In addition to wasting millions of tax dollars in court, the federal judiciary has also set prison population limits, forcing the early parole of thousands of violent offenders and consequently a rise in crime. Some Congressmen have pushed for amendments to the crime bill to restrain frivolous prison lawsuits, but Congress as a whole shows no willingness to limit the power of federal judges.

Crime bill follies. Jeff Rosen, *The New Republic* v210 p 22–5 Mr 21 '94

If passed, the Senate crime bill would have perverse consequences and would transform the relationship between the national and local governments. The most objectionable parts of the bill would federalize almost any state crime committed with a gun and would impose a series of new mandatory minimum federal sentences.

According to estimates, up to 600,000 new cases would become eligible for federal prosecution, and prosecuting these cases would cost $8 billion per year, $2 billion more than for all other federal offenses combined. Mandatory minimum sentences are already clogging the federal courts and crowding prison cells with nonviolent offenders, forcing the release of violent criminals. Other invidious crime bill elements would permanently lock up some third-time violent offenders and would impose federal death penalties for 54 new offenses. The bill's damage to federalism and civil rights could be minimized if the White House provided more leadership.

The incorrigibles. David A. Kaplan, *Newsweek* v121 p 48–50 Ja 18 '93

Society is struggling to protect itself from incorrigible sex offenders. Many random and repeat sexual predators are killers as well. Offenders who rape, molest, abuse, and terrorize without killing are spared execution or long prison sentences; instead, they do some time and then are set free, regardless of the dangers they may pose to society. Criminal law's toughest dilemma is determining how to balance society's need for protection against an individual's constitutional rights, given that people are put in prison for what they have done, not for what they might do. The writer describes 3 incorrigible criminals—Donald Chapman, Peter Anderson, and Earl Shriner—and discusses tough new sexual predator laws and therapy for sex offenders.

The violence in our heads. David Gelman, *Newsweek* v122 p 48–9 Ag 2 '93

Any attempt to understand teen violence should begin with a look at the culture of violence in which teens have been raised. In the last 30 years, Americans have developed a culture of violence so pervasive that it can be found in their speech, entertainment, and business styles. Debra Prothrow-Stith, an assistant dean at the Harvard School of Public Health, notes that a widespread "make my day" ethic expressed at different cultural levels may be largely to blame for both the rise in teen crime and its increasing callousness. According to psychiatrists, the constant repetition of the violent imagery found in movies and sports desensitizes people. Images are not reality, but it would be wrong to think that they have no impact on the young.

How America's meanest lobby ran out of ammo. Jonathan Alter, *Newsweek* v123 p 24–5 My 16 '94

The House of Representatives recently voted 216–214 to ban assault weapons, marking a shift in U.S. politics and an advance of the Clinton agenda. The National Rifle Association (NRA) is the most fearsome Washington lobby in the postwar era, but it became a useful target itself during this battle. Some politicians, for example, find that being attacked by the organization boosts their reputation for independence. The ban is notable for revealing a return to sanity and common sense in Congress: While it is acknowledged that the ban may not seriously reduce crime, legislators read the bill and made a conscientious decision, showing con-

stituents that they are taking steps to deal with crime. The NRA is still
enormously wealthy and powerful, but its increased militancy is a boon to
the Clinton strategy of dividing average gun owners from gun fanatics.

Rough justice. Bernice Kanner, *New York* v26 p 46–51 My 10 '93

Assistant District Attorney Cindy Elan is a frontline soldier in society's
inconsistent efforts to fight back against the disproportionate amount of
violence that occurs in the Bronx. Although the borough comprises only
16 percent of New York City's population, it is home to 22 percent of its
drug arrests, 25 percent of its homicides, and 20 percent of its rapes. Last
year, the number of felonies prosecuted in the Bronx totaled more than
10,000—an increase of more than 50 percent since 1985. Elan spends
each day dealing with this extraordinary violence and disorder even as she
tries to seek justice and maintain her idealism. The article discusses some
of her more famous cases.

The man who kept going free. Jeffrey R. Toobin, *The New Yorker* v70 p 38–48+ Mr 7 '94

Before he killed 12-year-old Polly Klaas, Richard Allen Davis was the
classic offender that the criminal-justice system couldn't keep in jail.
Davis, who had spent 14 of the last 20 years in jail, confessed to dozens of
crimes over the years. Virtually every time prosecutors went after him,
judges handed down stiff sentences, and parole boards, when they could,
denied him parole.

Nevertheless, loopholes in the system invariably allowed Davis to go
free. In the light of Klaas's murder, California and many other states are
poised to approved some version of "three strikes and you're out," which
would mandate life sentences for individuals convicted of three violent
felonies.

Drive to keep repeat felons in prison gains in California. Jane Gross, *New York Times* (Late New York Edition) p 1+ (Sec 1) D 26 '93

(Dec. 23) Mike Reynolds's personal crusade to tighten sentencing for career criminals has become a political juggernaut in California, where
several high-profile crimes have been in the spotlight in recent weeks.
Reynolds wrote a ballot measure that would double and triple sentences
and limit parole opportunities for chronic criminals like the one who
killed his teen-age daughter, Kimber. Petitions for the ballot measure are
being signed at the rate of 15,000 voters a day.

The campus crime wave. (cover story) Anne Matthews, *The New York Times Magazine* p 38–42+ Mr 7 '93

Increasing violence on college campuses has turned many schools into
discreetly armed camps. The average American college or university aver-

ages 3 reported violent assaults a year, 8 incidents of hate crimes or hazing violence, 430 property crimes, countless alcohol violations, and an indefinite number of rapes or sexual assaults. In response to the increase in crime, many schools have started using electronic passkeys for dormitories, cold-steel mesh on classroom windows, computer-controlled cameras in stairwells, and alarm strips in toilet stalls. In addition, the Campus Sexual Assault Victims' Bill of Rights became law in July 1992; a clarification of the Buckley Privacy Amendment gives victims of campus violence easier access to the previous criminal records of student perpetrators; and the Student Right-to-Know and Campus Security Act, the first national law to require disclosure of crime rates on federally funded campuses, has been enacted.

Sister Sympathy. Sue M. Halpern, *The New York Times Magazine* p 28+ My 9 '93

Sister Helen Prejean, founder of Pilgrimage for Life, which works for the abolition of the death penalty, ministers to killers on death row and to the families of the people that they've killed. Her forthcoming book Dead Man Walking: An Eyewitness Account of the Death Penalty in the United States profiles the men of death row in a way that does not flinch from their crimes.

Their crimes don't make them adults. Alex Kotlowitz, *The New York Times Magazine* p 40–1 F 13 '94

A blanket policy of sending children who have been accused of crimes, both violent and nonviolent, into the adult courts is grievously misguided. Children, whose personalities are still forming, are thought to be more open to rehabilitation than adults, but retribution rather than rehabilitation is the result, if not the objective, of adult courts, into which thousands of children have been sent. The assumption of those who advocate the law-and-order approach is that trying children as adults will deter crime. Adult crime has not necessarily been reduced by longer sentences, however, and there is often an unintended consequence of these transfer laws: Because criminal courts are already so overburdened, some judges in adult courts have shown a propensity to hand out lighter sentences to children than they might receive in juvenile court. Several specific criminal cases involving juveniles are highlighted.

What's hate got to do with it? Jacob Sullum, *Reason* v24 p 14–18 D '92

In recent years, 46 states have adopted hate-crime laws, most of which increase the penalties for existing offenses when the crimes are motivated by bigotry. Traditional defenders of the First Amendment are divided over these measures. According to supporters, hate-crime laws are aimed at suppressing not speech or ideas but a particularly dangerous kind of crime. These advocates argue that hate crimes should be punished more severely than other crimes because they do more harm—for example, by exacerbating intergroup tensions and intimidating particular groups. By creating a distinction based on motive, however, hate-crime laws almost inevitably punish people on the basis of their speech. Punishing criminals more harshly for being bigots is really no different from giving them extra punishment because of their political beliefs. Crimes may indeed be more morally reprehensible when they are motivated by hate, but this distinction cannot be written into the law.

The state of Michigan vs. Gary Fannon: a tragic miscarriage of justice continues Mike Sager, *Rolling Stone* p 51–3+ S 2 '93

Garry Fannon, who was sentenced in 1986 to life without possibility of parole under Michigan's mandatory-minimum laws for the sentencing of drug cases, has now spent 7 years in prison. Fannon was convicted on a first-offense charge of cocaine delivery after being lured into the drug trade at age 18 by a police detective who later left the force after he tested positive for cocaine. Fannon's life in Detroit's Ryan Regional Correctional Facility, the efforts of his mother and friends to free him, his television appearances, and the effects of the Michigan law are discussed.

Crime, race, and values James Q. Wilson, *Society* v30 p 90–3 N/D '92

The best way to reduce racism, whether real or imagined, is to reduce the black crime rate to equal the white crime rate. Policies aimed at doing this must address both the material problems (scarce jobs, too little capital formation, badly managed public-housing projects, a perverse welfare program, and an overburdened criminal system) and the cultural problems (racism, fear, despair, defiance, poor work habits, inadequate skills, and a preference for joining predatory gangs instead of accepting low-wage jobs) that plague the inner cities. These policies must start early in life, when character and expectations are formed; focus on young males, who are the perpetrators of crime, the fathers of illegitimate children, and the gang members; and make lawful alternatives more attractive than unlawful ones.

Danger in the safety zone Jill Smolowe, *Time* v142 p 28–32 Ag 23 '93

Violence in America is spreading beyond urban areas and into small towns. An epidemic of shooting sprees in malls, fast-food restaurants, and movie theaters this summer has created the perception that almost no place is safe anymore. Fear has led to booming sales in the security industry and the transformation of homes and public places into fortresses. Recently released FBI statistics show 2 different trends in crime rates:

Occurrences of violence in cities and towns with populations under 1 million are creeping upward, while such incidents are on the decline in the most populous urban enclaves. The widening of targets to include suburban and rural areas and the savageness of the crimes in the headlines have left Americans feeling more vulnerable. Across the country, people are sealing off their homes and neighborhoods with various security devices.

Gangs, guns, and school violence. Ronald D. Stephens, *USA Today* (Periodical) v122 p 29–32 Ja '94

Part of a special section on youth and violence. School crime and violence are problematic in America's rural, suburban, and urban communities. The easy availability of guns coupled with community gang activity and the influence of drugs or alcohol can lead to impulsive violence. According to the National Crime Survey, nearly 3,000,000 thefts and violent crimes occur on or near school campuses every year. About 50 percent of all violent crimes against youths aged 12–19 occur in school buildings, on school property, or on adjacent streets. Developing a comprehensive and systematic response to school violence is a difficult and complex undertaking. Methods by which communities can begin to cope with school violence are discussed.

Cost of crime: $674 billion. *U.S. News & World Report* v116 p 40–1, 68+ Ja 17 '94

Part of a special section on violent crime in the U.S. According to economists and criminal justice experts around the country, crime is costing the nation a staggering $674 billion a year. This figure represents the combined costs of federal, state, and local spending on police, prisons, and the court system; citizens' and companies' spending on private protection; and lost wages and productivity due to homicide, rape, burglary, and assault. An editorial notes that Americans are fed up with paying such a high toll and want criminals punished far more severely than they are now. Methods of raising the certainty of criminal punishment are discussed.

Domestic terrorism. Donna Shalala, *Vital Speeches of the Day* v60 p 450–3 My 15 '94

The Secretary of Health and Human Services addresses the AMA National Conference on Family Violence in Washington, DC: Domestic violence is an unacknowledged epidemic in the U.S. Every year, about four million women in the U.S. become victims of this crime. In 1994, for the first time ever, the Clinton administration and Congress allocated funds to the CDC with the aim of investigating and reducing violence against women. In addition, the Senate-passed version of the crime bill contains the Violence

Against Women Act, which would authorize $1.8 billion over 5 years to aid police, prosecutors, women's shelters, and community-prevention programs and to set up a national hotline for victims of domestic abuse. The AMA's guidelines for diagnosing the abuse of children, women, and the elderly are monumental achievements. Americans must do more, however, to elevate the issue to the national stage.